EASY PIANO

SIMPLE SONGS

THE EASIEST EASY PIANO SONGS

ISBN 978-1-4950-1123-8

HAL•LEONARD®
CORPORATION

7777 W. BLUEMOUND RD. P.O. BOX 13819 MILWAUKEE, WI 53213

AU CLAIR DE LA LUNE

French Folksong

THE ASH GROVE

Old Welsh Air

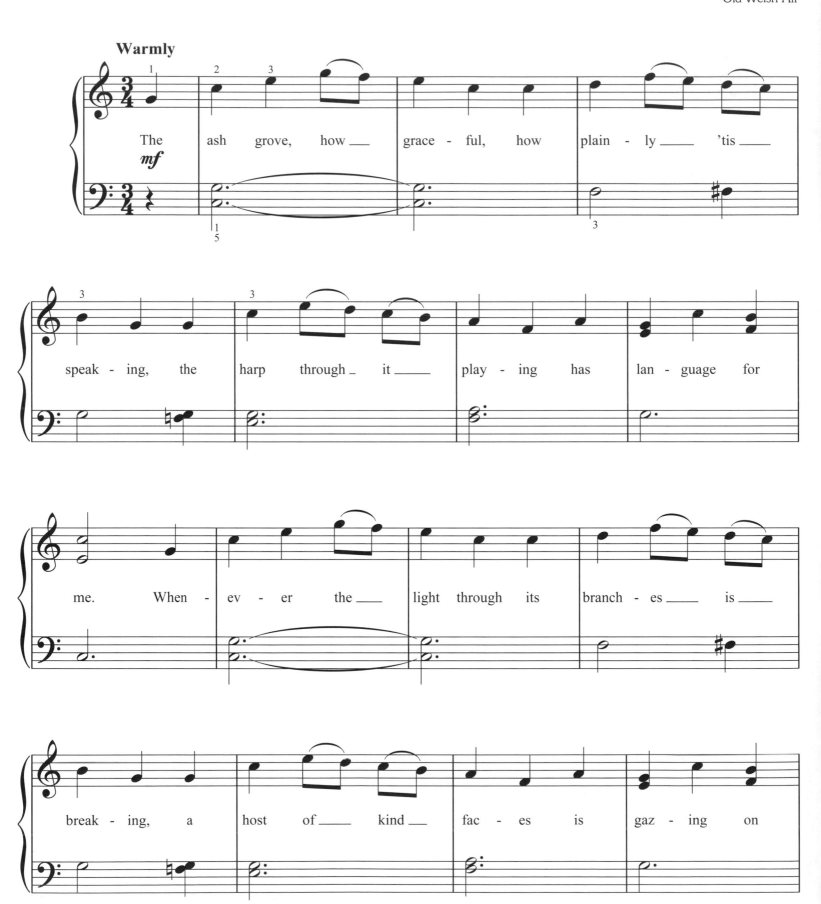

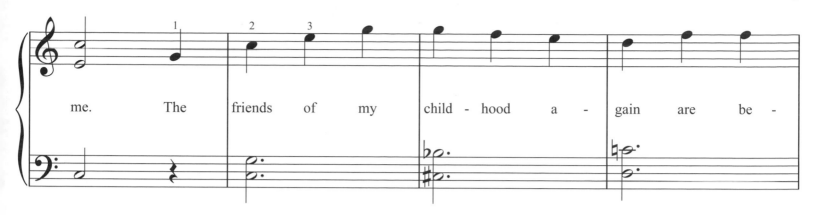

me. The friends of my child - hood a - gain are be -

fore me, each step wakes a mem - 'ry, as free - ly I

roam. With soft whis - pers ___ la - den, its leaves rus - tle ___

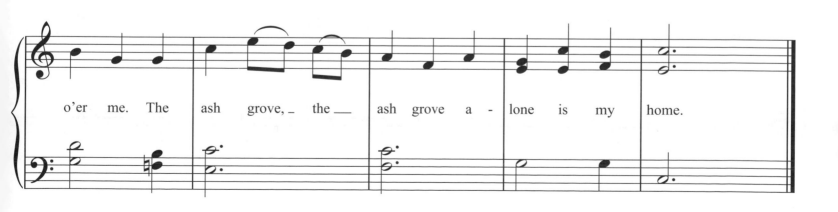

o'er me. The ash grove, _ the _ ash grove a - lone is my home.

AULD LANG SYNE

Words by ROBERT BURNS
Traditional Scottish Melody

Slowly

Should auld ac-quaint-ance be for-got, and nev - er brought to

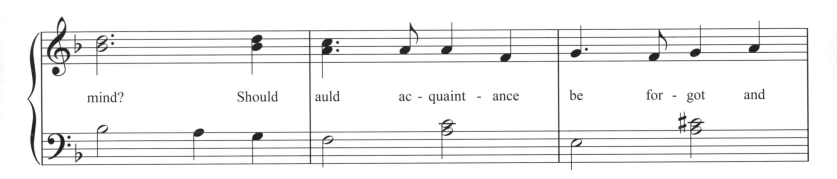

mind? Should auld ac - quaint - ance be for - got and

days of auld lang syne? For auld _____ lang _____

syne, my dear, for auld _____ lang _____ syne, we'll

take a cup of kind - ness yet, for ___ auld ___ lang ___

syne. For auld ___ lang ___ syne, my dear, for

auld ___ lang ___ syne, we'll take a cup of

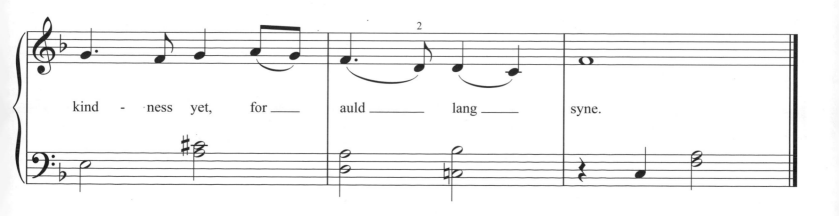

kind - ness yet, for ___ auld ___ lang ___ syne.

BEAUTY AND THE BEAST
from Walt Disney's BEAUTY AND THE BEAST

Music by ALAN MENKEN
Lyrics by HOWARD ASHMAN

Slowly

mf

Tale as old as time,
Tale as old as time,

true as it can
tune as old as

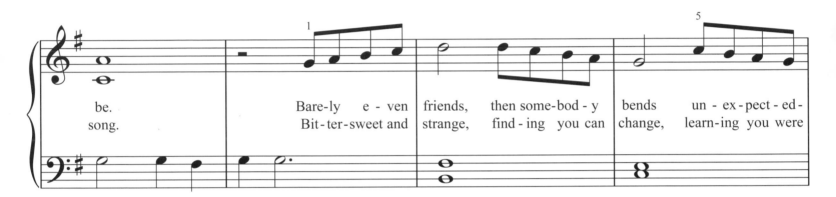

be.
song.

Bare-ly e - ven friends, then some-bod - y bends un - ex - pect - ed-
Bit - ter-sweet and strange, find - ing you can change, learn-ing you were

ly.
wrong.

Just a lit - tle change,
Cer-tain as the sun

small, to say the
ris - ing in the

least. Both a lit - tle scared, nei - ther one pre - pared. }
East. Tale as old as time, song as old as rhyme. }

Beau - ty and the

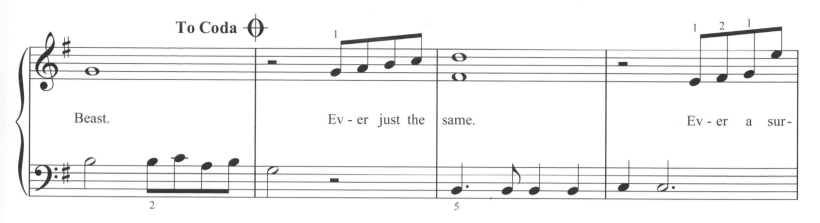

Beast.　　　　　　Ev - er just the　same.　　　　　　Ev - er a sur-

prise.　　　　　　Ev - er as be - fore,　　　ev - er just as

sure　　　as the sun will　rise.

Tale as old as

time,　　song as old as　rhyme,　Beau-ty and the　Beast.

BEYOND THE SEA

Lyrics by JACK LAWRENCE
Music by CHARLES TRENET and ALBERT LASRY
Original French Lyric to "La Mer" by CHARLES TRENET

be - yond a star; it's near be - yond the

moon. _____ I know _____ be - yond a

D.S. al Coda

doubt, my heart will lead me there soon. _____ We'll

CODA

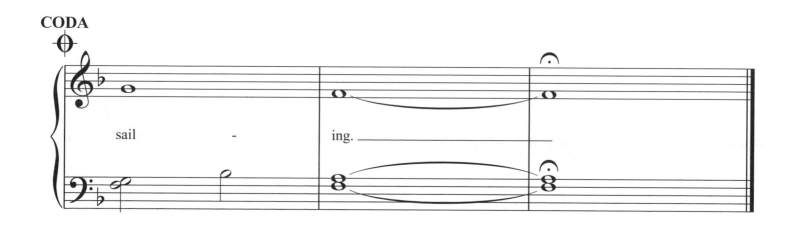

sail - ing. _____

BLUE SKIES

from BETSY

Words and Music by
IRVING BERLIN

Moderately

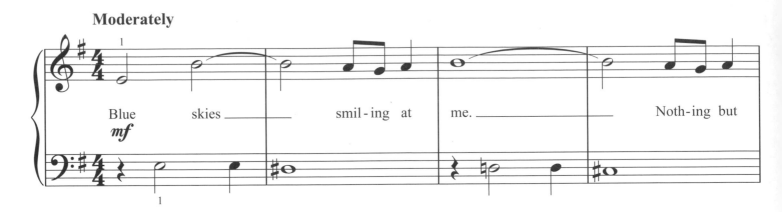

Blue skies ____ smil-ing at me. ____ Noth-ing but

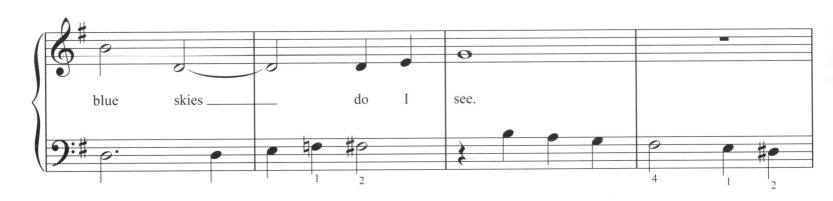

blue skies ____ do I see.

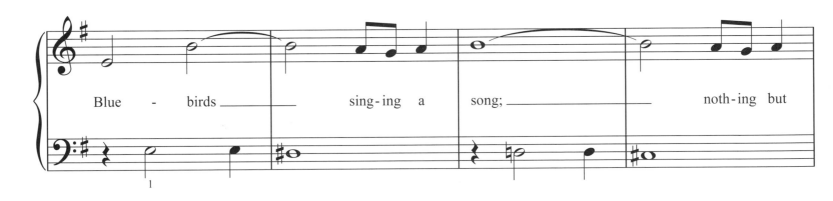

Blue - birds ____ sing-ing a song; ____ noth-ing but

blue - birds ____ all day long. ____

Nev - er saw the sun shin-ing so bright. Nev - er saw things go - ing so right.

No - tic - ing the days hur - ry - ing by; when you're in love, my, how they fly.

Blue days, all of them gone. Noth-ing but

blue skies from now on.

CASTLE ON A CLOUD
from LES MISÉRABLES

Music by CLAUDE-MICHEL SCHÖNBERG
Lyrics by ALAIN BOUBLIL, JEAN-MARC NATEL
and HERBERT KRETZMER

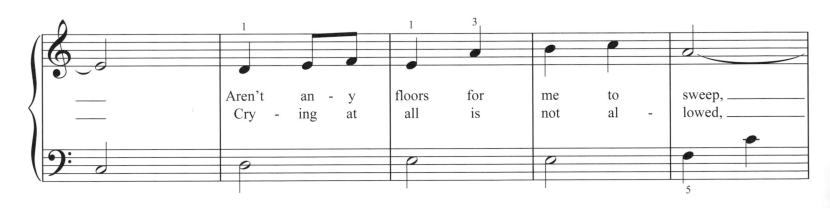

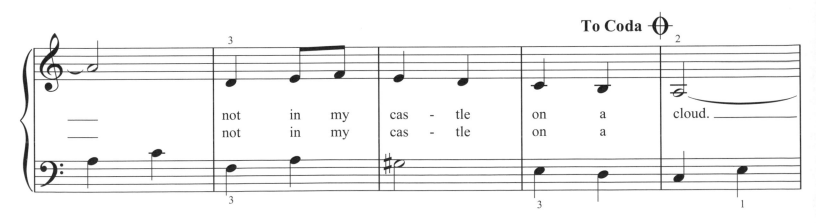

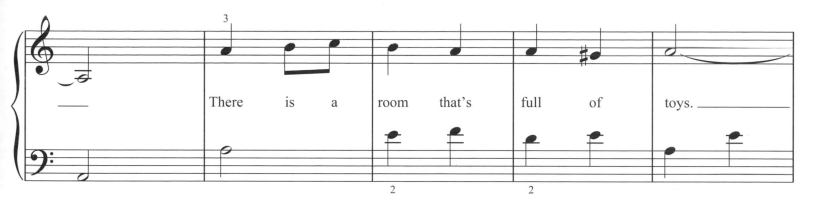

There is a room that's full of toys.

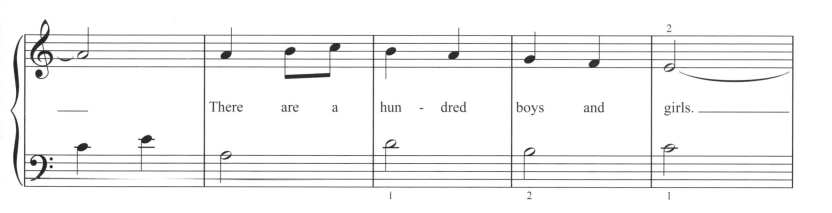

There are a hun - dred boys and girls.

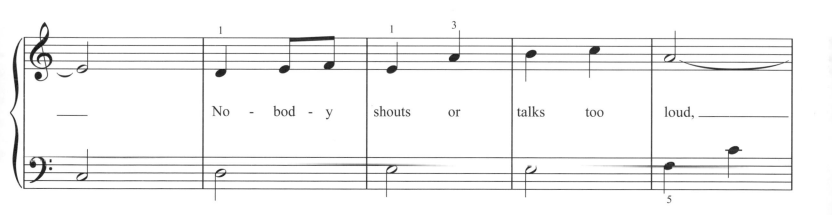

No - bod - y shouts or talks too loud,

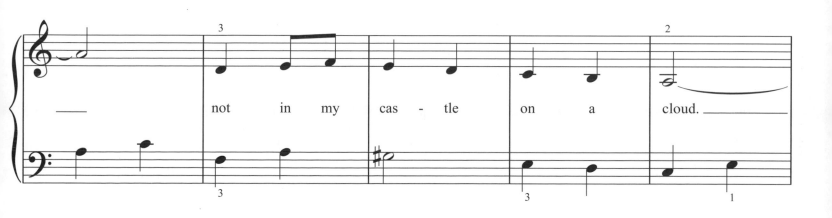

not in my cas - tle on a cloud.

There is a la - dy all in white, _____

holds me and sings a lull - a - by. She's nice to

see and she's soft to touch. She says, "Co - sette, I
rit.

D.C. al Coda

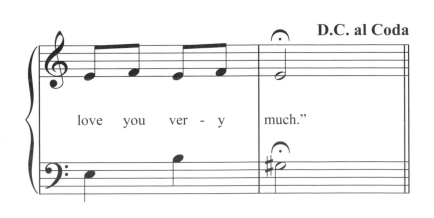

love you ver - y much."

CODA

cloud. _____

CAN YOU FEEL THE LOVE TONIGHT

from Walt Disney Pictures' THE LION KING

Music by ELTON JOHN
Lyrics by TIM RICE

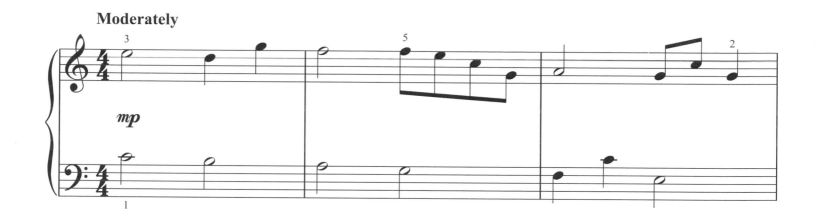

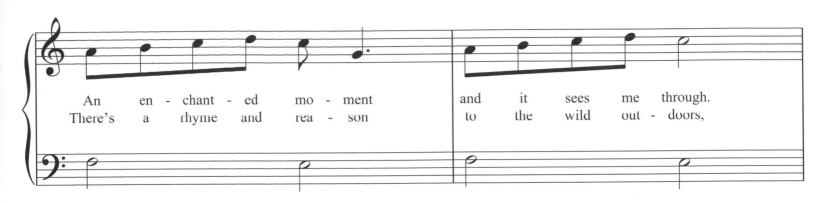

An en - chant - ed mo - ment and it sees me through.
There's a rhyme and rea - son to the wild out - doors,

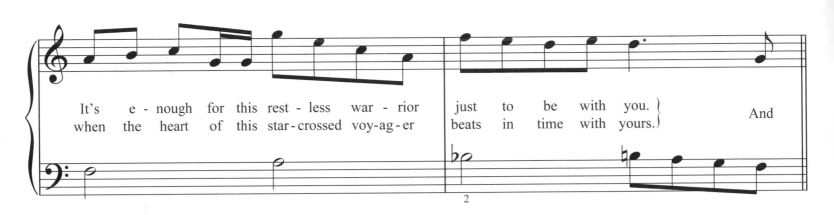

It's e - nough for this rest - less war - rior just to be with you. And
when the heart of this star - crossed voy - ag - er beats in time with yours.

can you feel the love to - night? _ It is where we
can you feel the love to - night? _ How it's laid to

are. It's e - nough for this wide - eyed wan - der - er
rest? It's e - nough to make kings and va - ga - bonds be -

that we got this far. And lieve the ver - y best. __

To Coda ⊕

D.S. al Coda
(take repeat)

CODA
⊕

It's e-nough to make

kings and vag - a - bonds be - lieve the ver - y best. __

rit. e dim.

CATCH A FALLING STAR

Words and Music by PAUL VANCE
and LEE POCKRISS

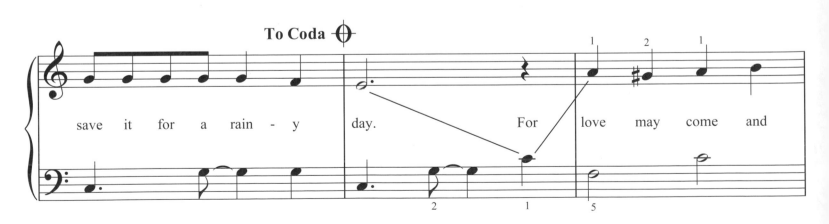

tap you on the shoul - der,   some star - less   night.   And

just in case you   feel you want to hold her,   you'll have a

D.C. al Coda

CODA

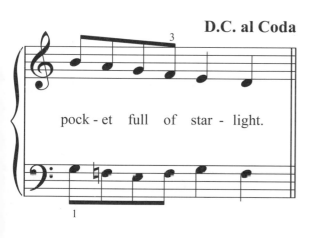

pock - et full of star - light.

day.   Save it for a

rain - y day.

CHOPSTICKS

By ARTHUR DE LULLI

DO-RE-MI
from THE SOUND OF MUSIC

Lyrics by OSCAR HAMMERSTEIN II
Music by RICHARD RODGERS

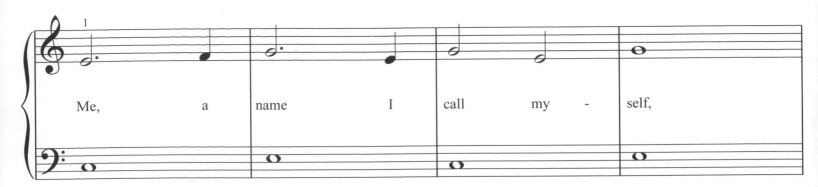

Me, a name I call my - self,

far, a long, long way to run. _____

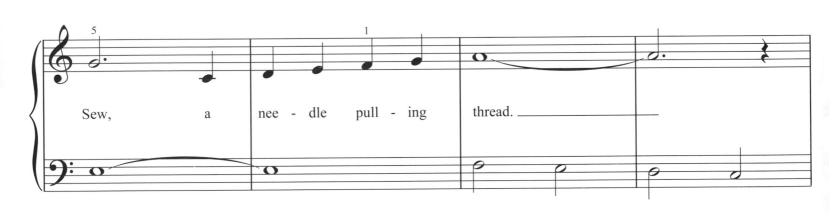

Sew, a nee - dle pull - ing thread. _____

La, a note to fol - low sew. _____

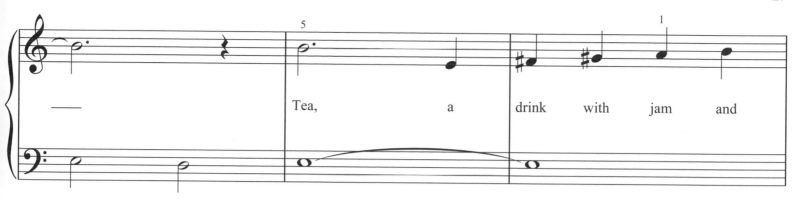

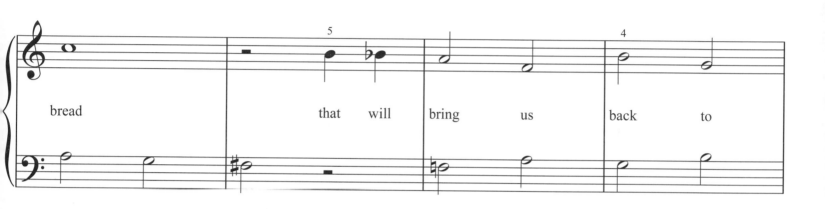

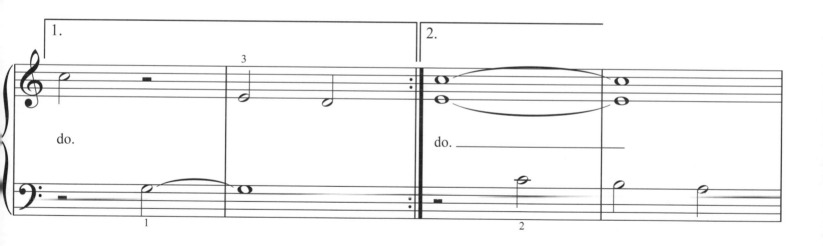

GREENSLEEVES

Sixteenth Century Traditional English

HAPPY BIRTHDAY TO YOU

Words and Music by MILDRED J. HILL
and PATTY S. HILL

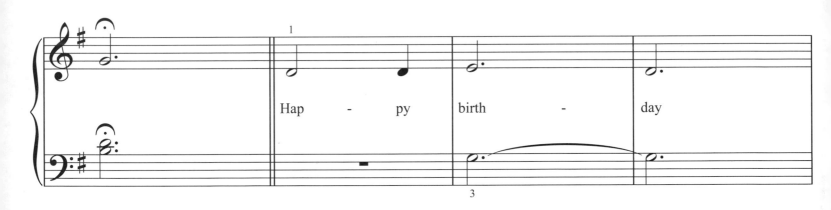

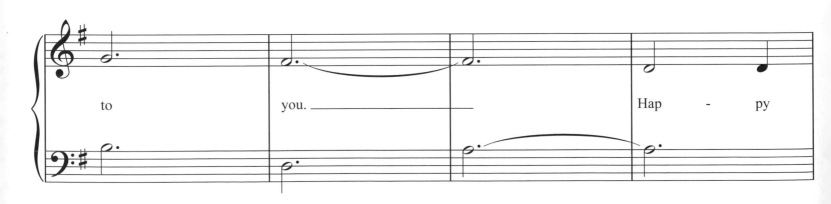

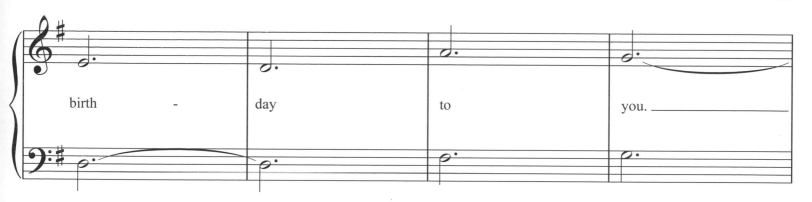

birth - day to you. _____

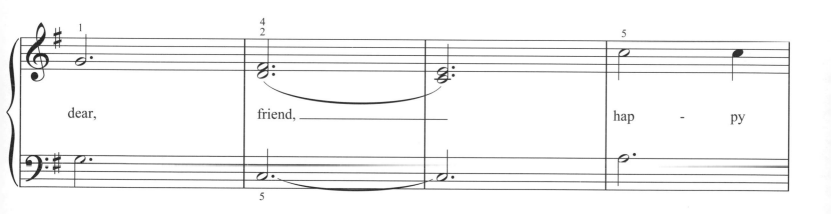

_____ Hap - py birth - day,

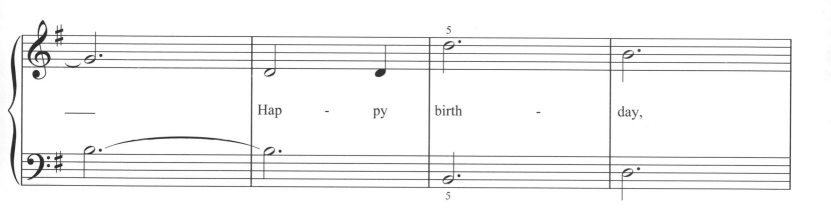

dear, friend, _____ hap - py

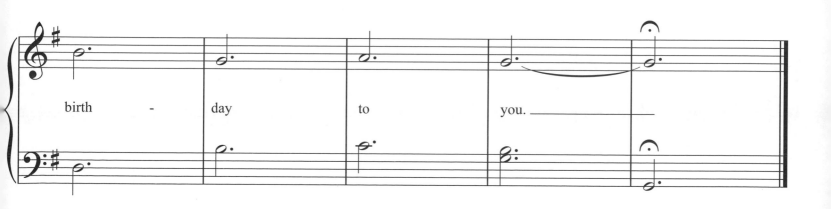

birth - day to you. _____

HE'S A PIRATE

from Walt Disney Pictures' PIRATES OF THE CARIBBEAN:
THE CURSE OF THE BLACK PEARL

Music by KLAUS BADELT

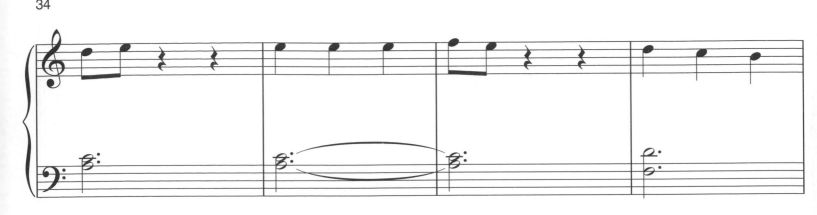

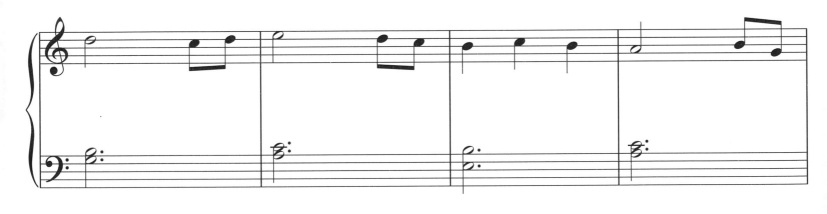

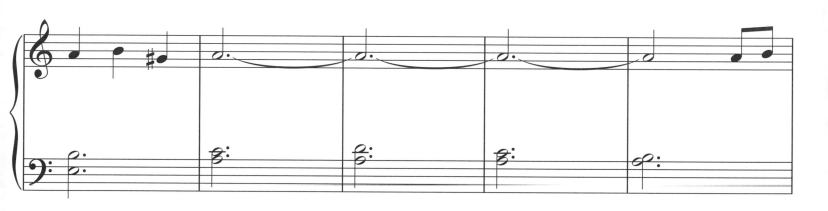

IN THE MOOD

By JOE GARLAND

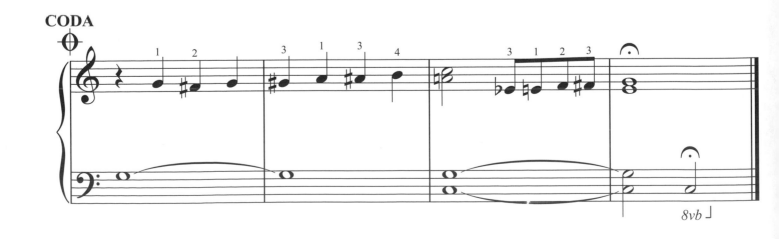

HEY JUDE

Words and Music by JOHN LENNON
and PAUL McCARTNEY

min - ute you let her un - der your skin, then you be - gin ___
mem - ber to let her in - to your heart; then you can start ___

___ to make it ___ bet - ter. An - y time you feel the
___ to make it ___ bet - ter. Let it out and let it

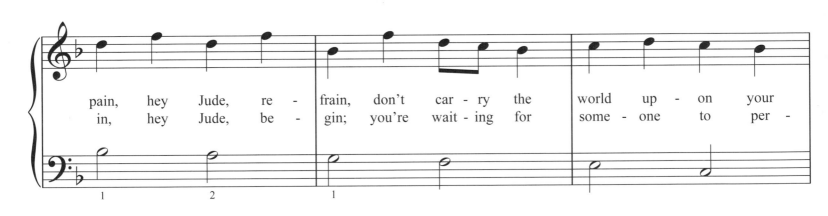

pain, hey Jude, re - frain, don't car - ry the world up - on your
in, hey Jude, be - gin; you're wait - ing for some - one to per -

shoul - ders. ___ Well, you know that it's a fool who plays it
form with. ___ Don't you know that it's just you, hey Jude, you'll

cool, by mak - ing his world a lit - tle cold - er. ____ } Da da
do, the move-ment you need is on your shoul - der. ____ }

da da da da da da. Hey da. Hey

D.S. al Coda

CODA

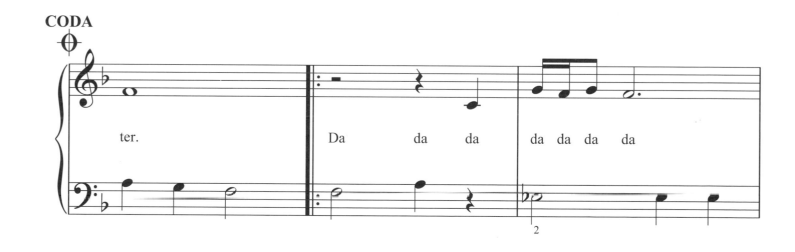

ter. Da da da da da da da

da da da da hey ____ Jude. Jude.

LET IT GO
from Disney's Animated Feature FROZEN

Music and Lyrics by KRISTEN ANDERSON-LOPEZ
and ROBERT LOPEZ

Half-time feel

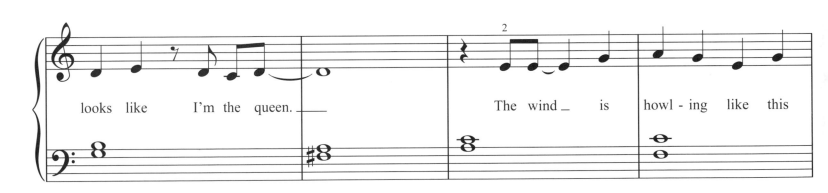

heav - en knows I ____ tried.   Don't let ____ them

in,   don't   let   them   see,   be   the   good   girl   you   al - ways   have   to

be.   Con - ceal,   don't   feel,   don't   let   them   know...   Well, now ___

____   they   know. ___   Let   it   go, ___   let   it   go, ___   can't ___

hold it back an-y-more. _____ Let it go, _____ let it go, _____

_____ turn a-way _____ and slam _ the _ door. I don't _ care _

_____ what they're going to _ say, _____ let the storm rage _ on.

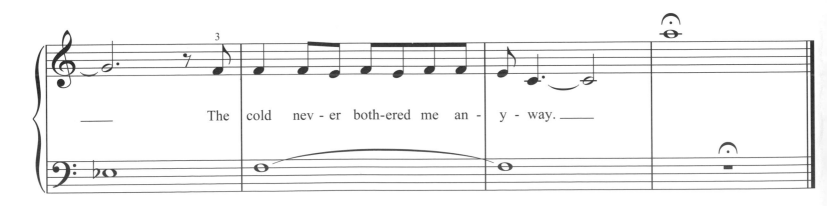

_____ The cold nev-er both-ered me an-y-way. _____

IMAGINE

Words and Music by
JOHN LENNON

day. Ah. _____ I - mag - ine there's no coun - tries.
                                                    sions.

It is - n't hard to do. ___
I won - der if you can. ___

Noth - ing to kill or die
No need for greed or hun -

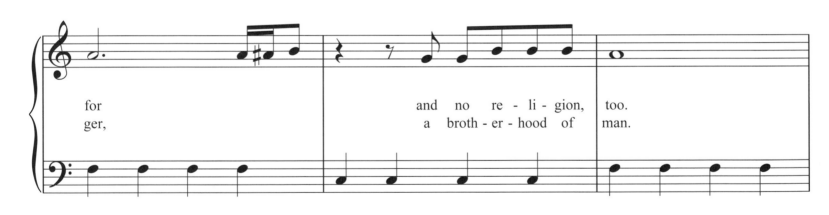

for
ger,

and no re - li - gion, too.
a broth - er - hood of man.

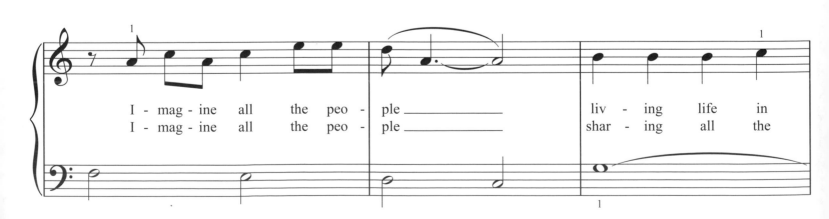

I - mag - ine all the peo - ple _____
I - mag - ine all the peo - ple _____

liv - ing life in
shar - ing all the

peace.
world. You, _____ you may say I'm a dream - er.

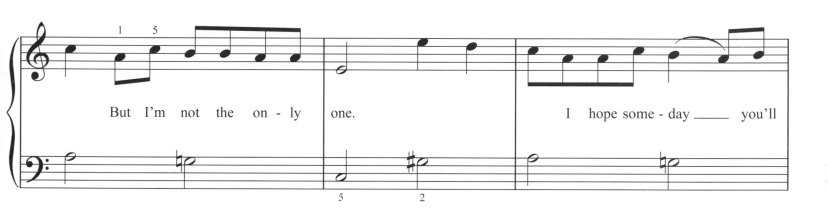

But I'm not the on - ly one. I hope some - day _____ you'll

1.

join us _____ and the world _____ will be as one.

2.

I - mag - ine no pos - ses - and the world _____ will be as one.

LET IT BE

Words and Music by JOHN LENNON
and PAUL McCARTNEY

Slowly

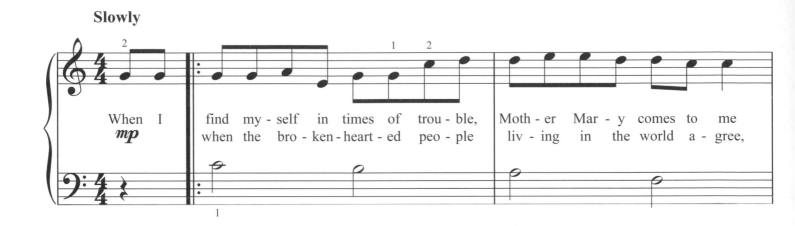

When I find my-self in times of trou-ble,
when the bro-ken-heart-ed peo-ple

Moth-er Mar-y comes to me
liv-ing in the world a-gree,

speak-ing words of wis-dom; let it be. _____ And
there will be an an-swer, let it be. _____ For

in my hour of dark-ness, she is
though they may be part-ed there is

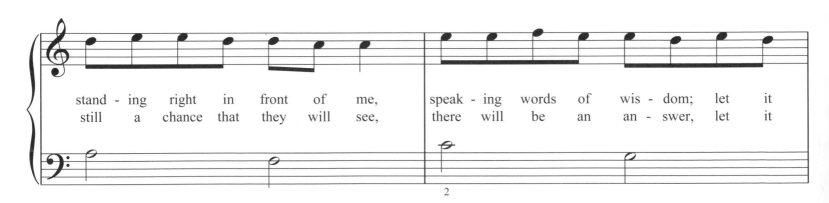

stand-ing right in front of me,
still a chance that they will see,

speak-ing words of wis-dom; let it
there will be an an-swer, let it

be. _____ } Let it be, let it be, let it be, let it be.

Whis-per words of wis-dom; let it be. _____ And be. _____ Let it

be, let it be, let it be, let it be. Whis-per words of wis-dom; let it

be _____   *rit.*

LINUS AND LUCY

By VINCE GUARALDI

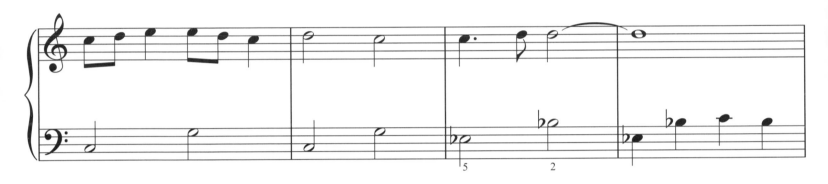

LONG, LONG AGO

By THOMAS BAYLY

Moderately

Tell me the tales that to me were so dear

mf

long, long a - go, long, long a - go.

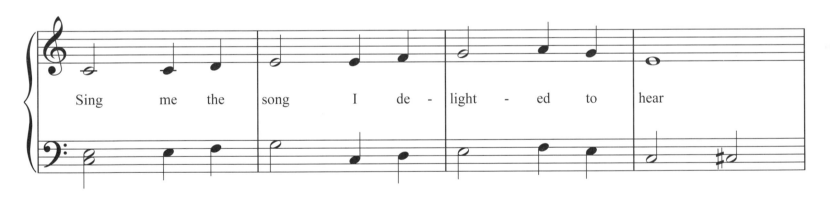

Sing me the song I de - light - ed to hear

long, long a - go, long a - go. ____

Now you are come all my grief is re - moved,

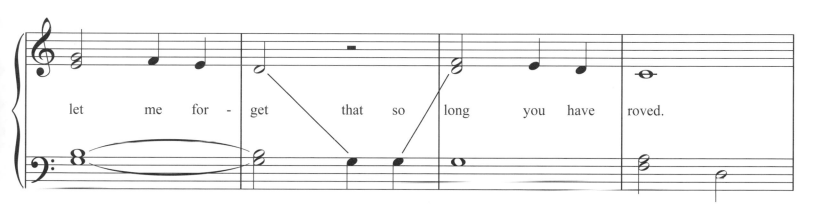

let me for - get that so long you have roved.

Let me be - lieve that you love as you loved,

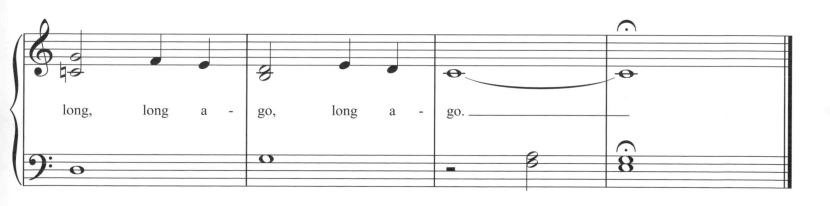

long, long a - go, long a - go.

LOVE ME TENDER

Words and Music by ELVIS PRESLEY
and VERA MATSON

Flowing

mf Love me ten - der, love me sweet; nev - er let me go.
Love me ten - der, love me dear; tell me you are mine.

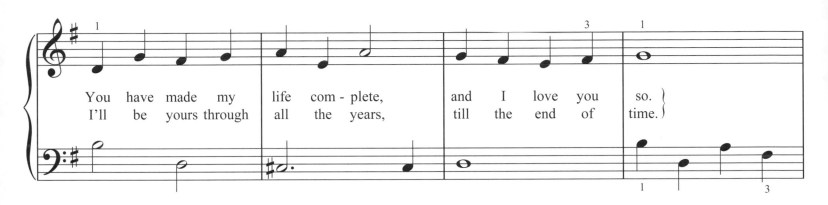

You have made my life com - plete, and I love you so.
I'll be yours through all the years, till the end of time.

Love me ten - der, love me true, all my dreams ful - fill. For, my dar - lin',

1. I love you, and I al - ways will.
2. and I al - ways will.

MEMORY
from CATS

Music by ANDREW LLOYD WEBBER
Text by TREVOR NUNN after T.S. ELIOT

Flowing, in one

56

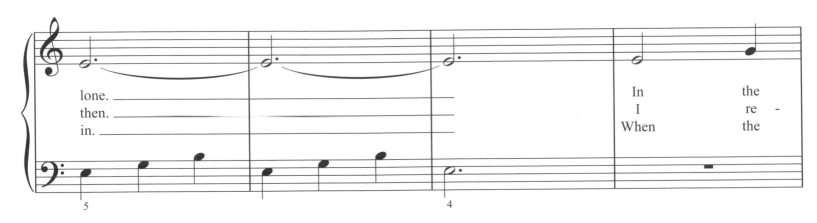

To Coda ⊕

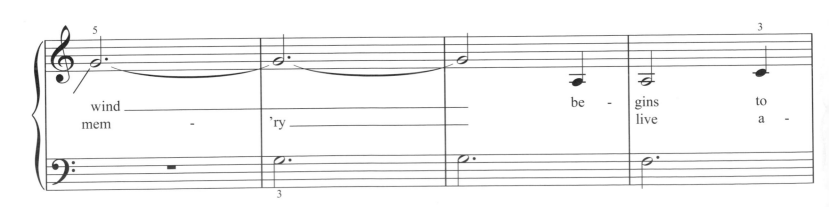

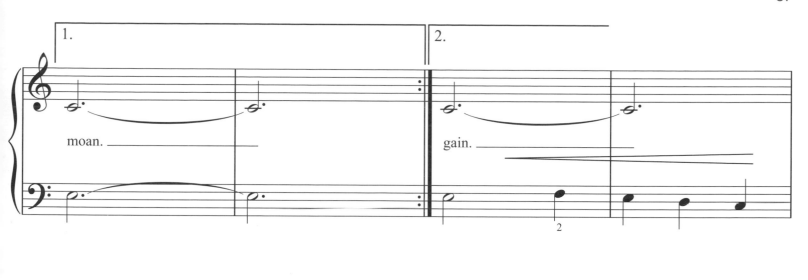

moan. | gain.

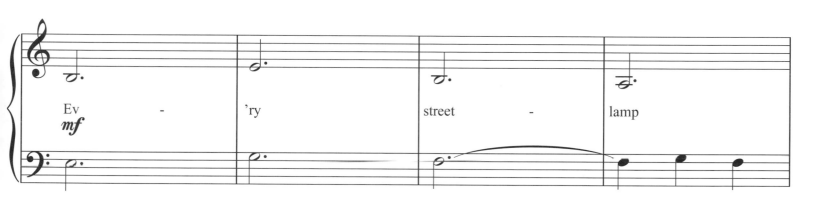

Ev - 'ry street - lamp

mf

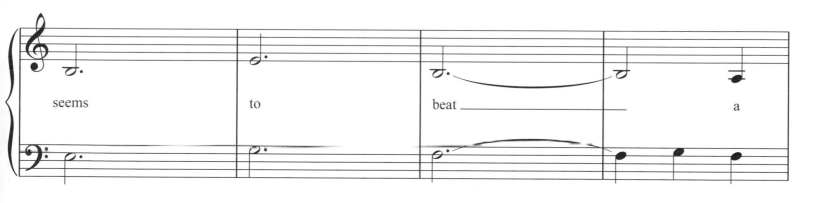

seems to beat a

fa - tal - is - tic

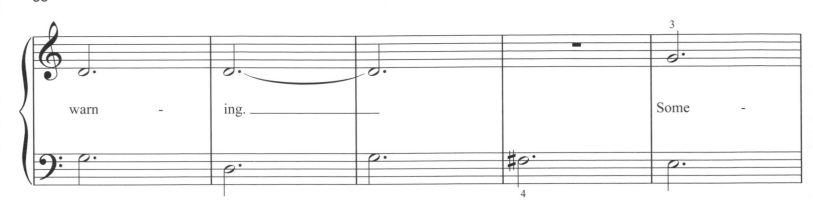

warn - ing. _____ Some -

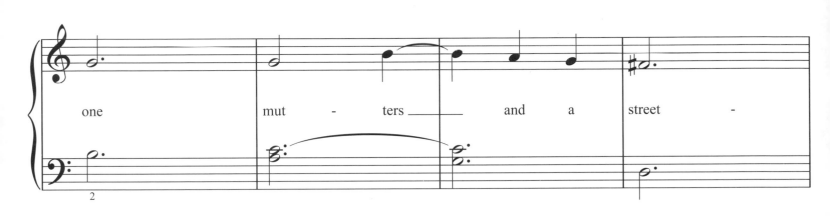

one mut - ters _____ and a street -

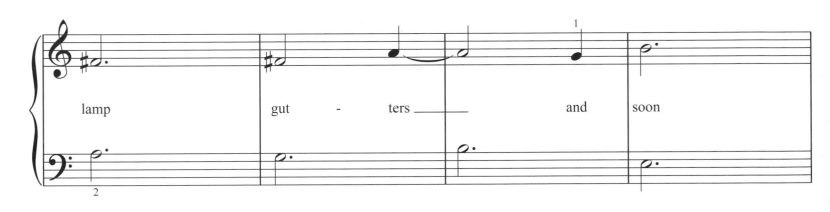

lamp gut - ters _____ and soon

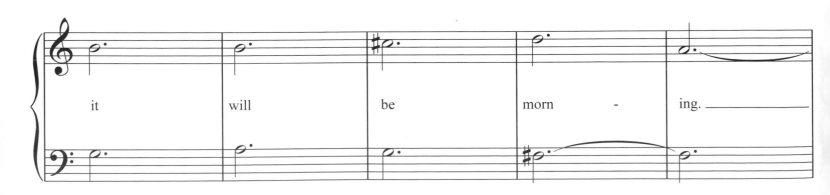

it will be morn - ing. _____

MISTY

Words by JOHNNY BURKE
Music by ERROLL GARNER

want you to do. _____ Don't you no - tice how help - less - ly I'm lost, _____

_____ that's why I'm fol - low-ing you. _____ On my own, would I

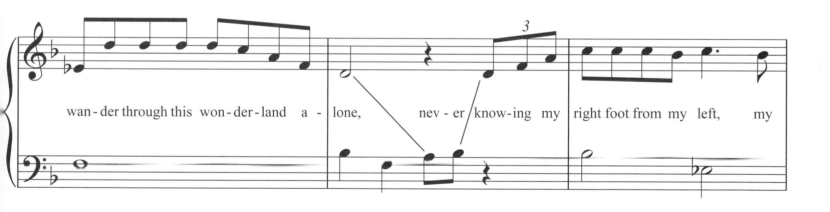

wan - der through this won - der - land a - lone, nev - er know-ing my right foot from my left, my

hat from my glove? I'm too mist - y and too much in love. _____
rit.

MOON RIVER

from the Paramount Picture BREAKFAST AT TIFFANY'S

Words by JOHNNY MERCER
Music by HENRY MANCINI

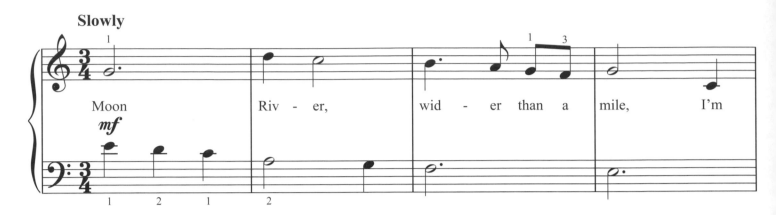

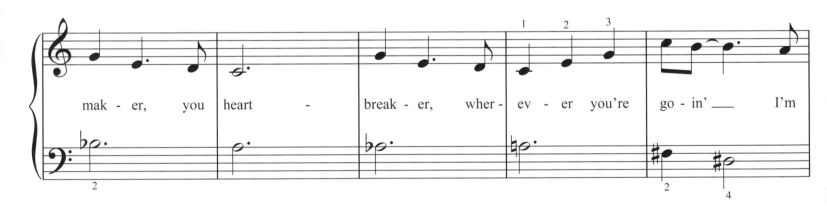

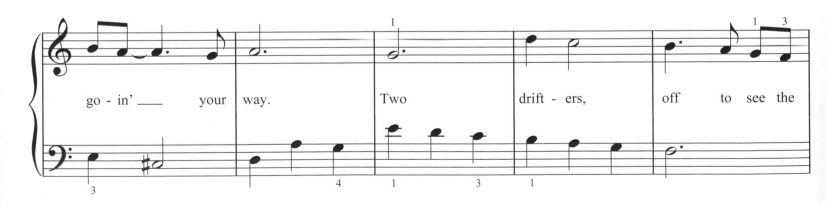

world. There's such a lot of world to see. _____ We're

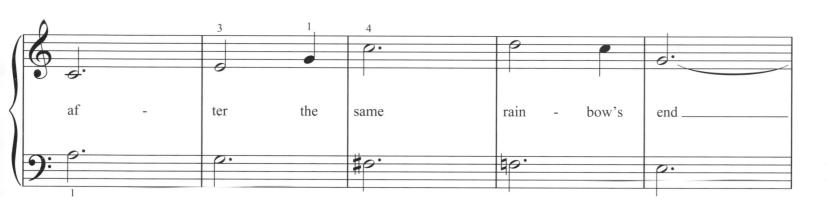

af - ter the same rain - bow's end _____

_____ wait - in' 'round the bend, _____ my huck - le - ber - ry friend,

Moon Riv - er _____ and me. _____

MY FAVORITE THINGS

from THE SOUND OF MUSIC

Lyrics by OSCAR HAMMERSTEIN II
Music by RICHARD RODGERS

Rain - drops on
Cream col - ored

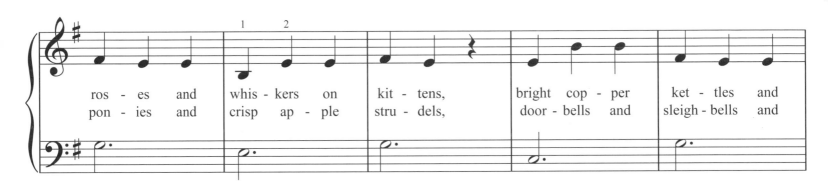

ros - es   and   whis - kers   on   kit - tens,   bright cop - per   ket - tles   and
pon - ies   and   crisp ap - ple   stru - dels,   door - bells and   sleigh - bells and

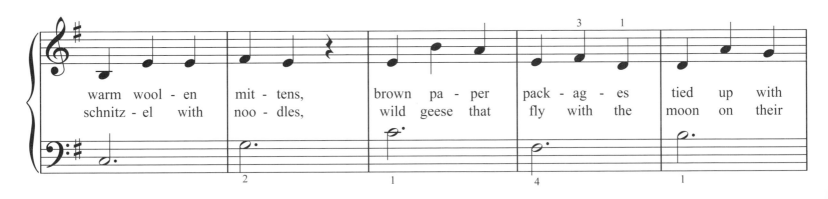

warm wool - en   mit - tens,   brown pa - per   pack - ag - es   tied   up   with
schnitz - el with   noo - dles,   wild geese that   fly with the   moon on their

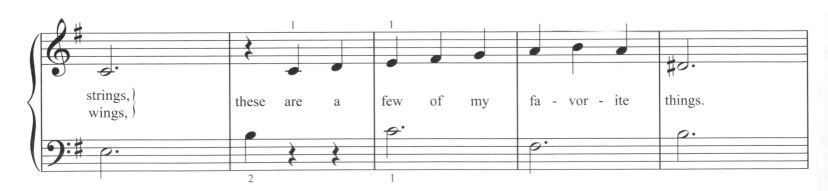

strings,
wings,   these are a   few of my   fa - vor - ite   things.

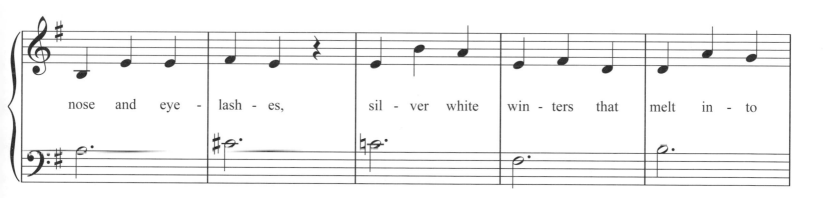

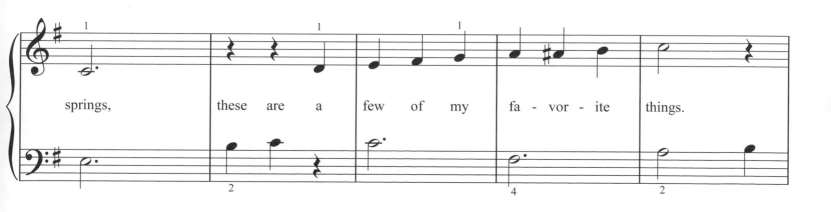

When the dog bites, when the bee stings, when I'm

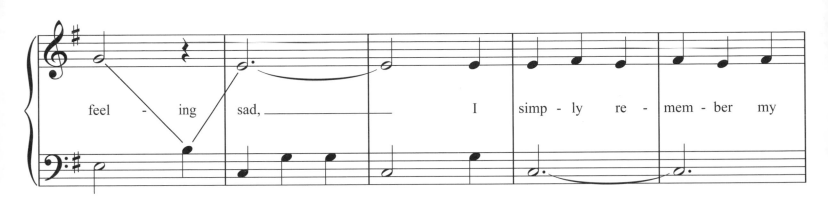

feel - ing sad, _____ I simp - ly re - mem - ber my

fa - vor - ite things and then I don't feel

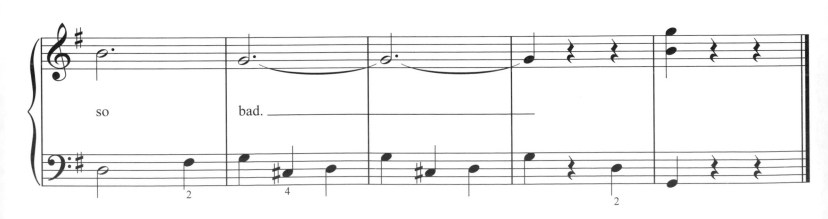

so bad. _____

ODE TO JOY

By LUDWIG VAN BEETHOVEN

MY FUNNY VALENTINE

from BABES IN ARMS

Words by LORENZ HART
Music by RICHARD RODGERS

My fun - ny Val - en - tine, sweet com - ic Val - en - tine,

you make me smile with my heart. Your looks are

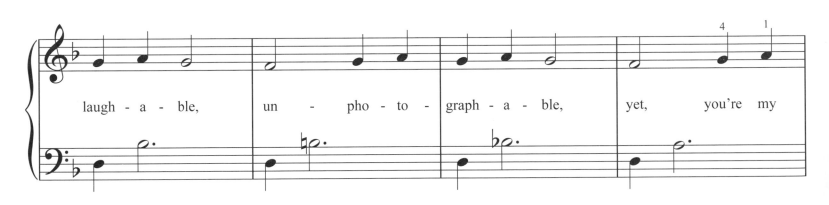

laugh - a - ble, un - pho - to - graph - a - ble, yet, you're my

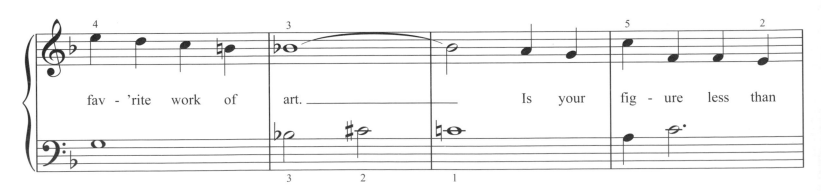

fav - 'rite work of art. _____ Is your fig - ure less than

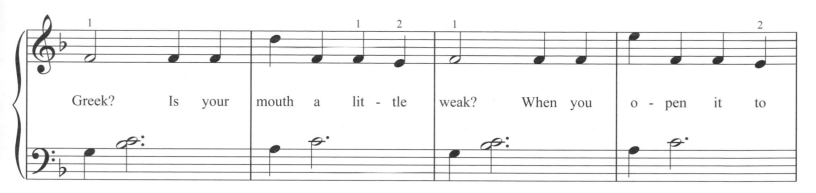

Greek? Is your mouth a lit - tle weak? When you o - pen it to

speak, are you smart? _____ But don't change a hair for me,

not if you care for me, stay, lit - tle Val - en - tine, stay! _____

_____ Each day is Val - en - tine's Day. _____

OH, WHAT A BEAUTIFUL MORNIN'
from OKLAHOMA!

Lyrics by OSCAR HAMMERSTEIN II
Music by RICHARD RODGERS

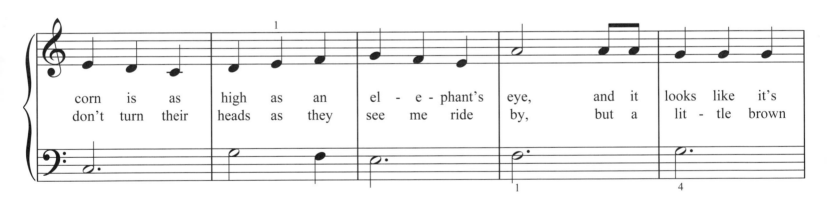

morn - in', oh, what a beau - ti - ful day. ____

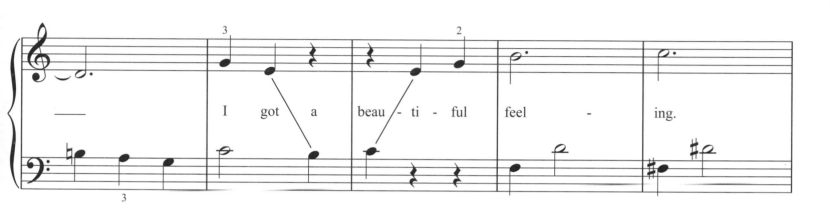

____ I got a beau - ti - ful feel - ing.

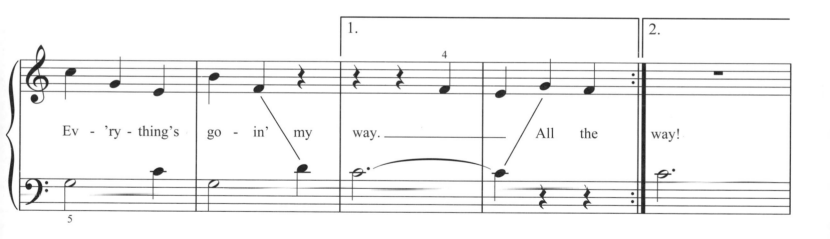

1.

Ev - 'ry - thing's go - in' my way. ____ All the

2.

way!

Oh, what a beau - ti - ful day. ____

71

ON MY OWN
from LES MISÉRABLES

Music by CLAUDE-MICHEL SCHÖNBERG
Lyrics by ALAIN BOUBLIL, JEAN-MARC NATEL,
HERBERT KRETZMER, JOHN CAIRD
and TREVOR NUNN

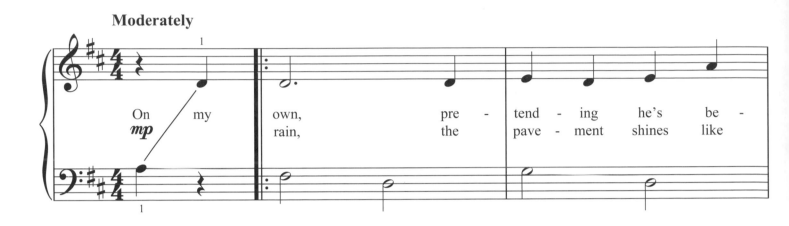

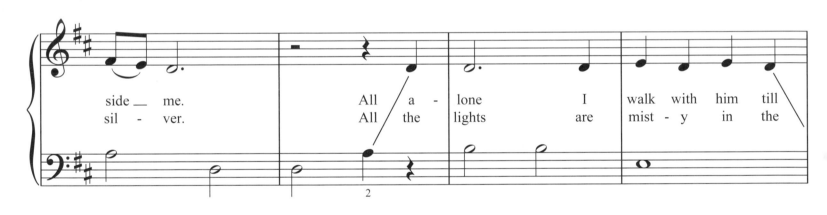

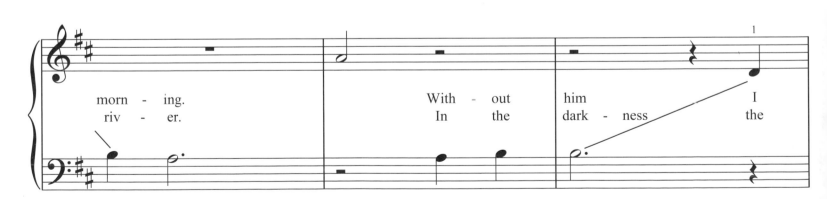

feel his arms a - round me. And when I lose my way I close my
trees are full of star - light. And all I see is him and me for -

eyes and he has found me. In the
ev - er and for - ev - er. And I

know it's on - ly in my mind that I'm

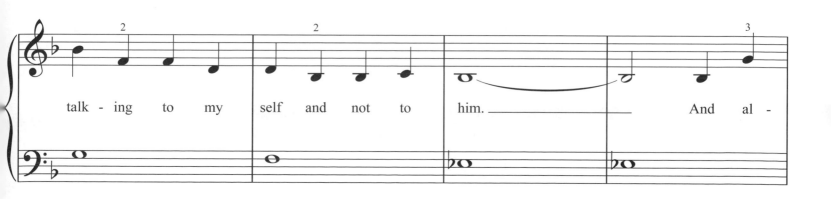

talk - ing to my self and not to him. _____ And al -

though I know that he is blind, still I

say there's a way for us. I

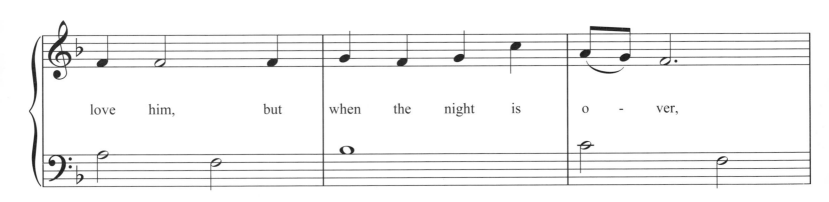

love him, but when the night is o - ver,

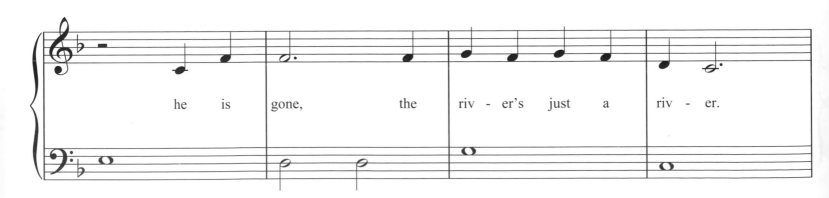

he is gone, the riv - er's just a riv - er.

With - out him, the world a - round me chang - es. The

trees are bare and ev - 'ry - where the streets are full of stran - gers.

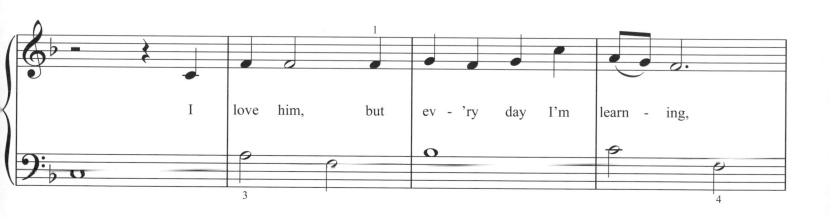

I love him, but ev - 'ry day I'm learn - ing,

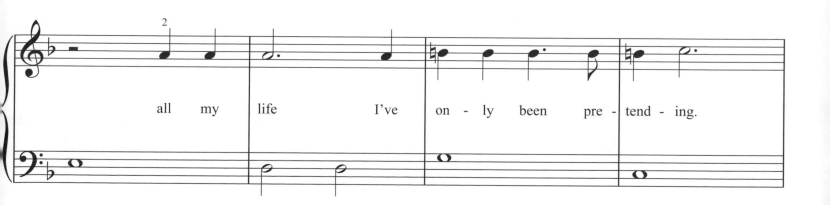

all my life I've on - ly been pre - tend - ing.

With - out me, his world will go on turn - ing. The

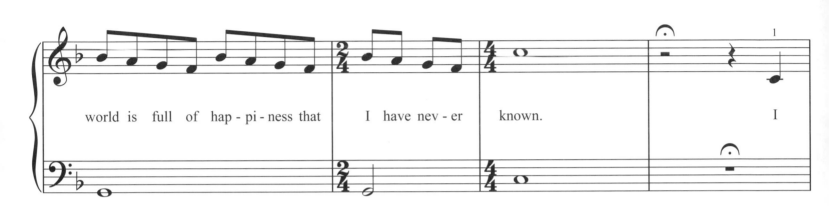

world is full of hap - pi - ness that I have nev - er known. I

Slower

love him, _____ I love him, _____ I

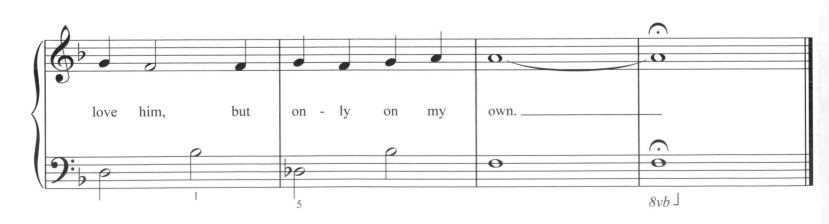

love him, but on - ly on my own. _____

8vb

OVER THE RAINBOW

from THE WIZARD OF OZ

Music by HAROLD ARLEN
Lyric by E.Y. "YIP" HARBURG

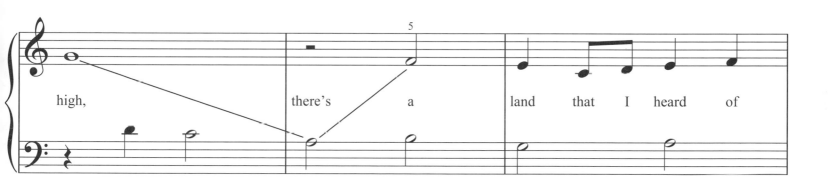

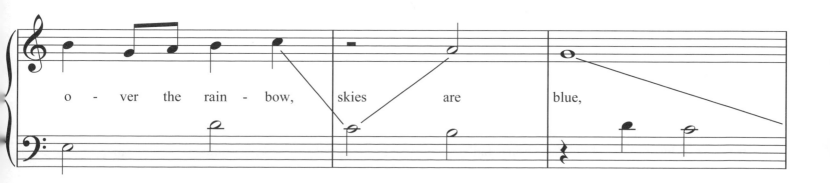

and the dreams that you dare to dream real - ly do come

true. Some - day I'll wish up - on a star and wake up where the clouds are far be -

hind me. Where trou - bles melt like lem - on drops, a -

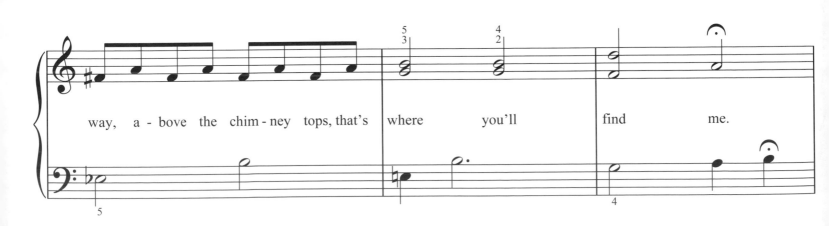

way, a - bove the chim - ney tops, that's where you'll find me.

Some - where   o - ver the rain - bow   blue - birds

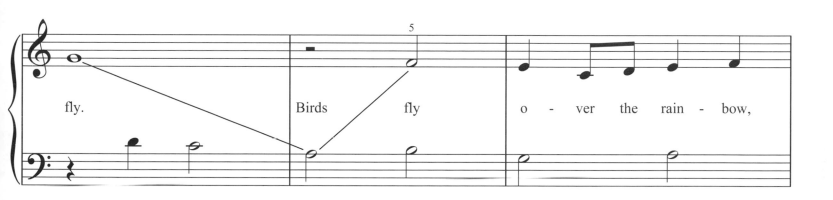

fly.   Birds   fly   o - ver the rain - bow,

why   then, oh, why   can't   I?   If   hap - py lit - tle blue-birds fly be -

yond   the rain - bow, why,   oh,   why can't   I?   *rit.*

POP GOES THE WEASEL

Traditional

Moderately

All a-round the cob - bler's bench, the mon - key chased the wea - sel. The

mon - key thought 'twas all ___ in fun. Pop, goes the wea - sel. A

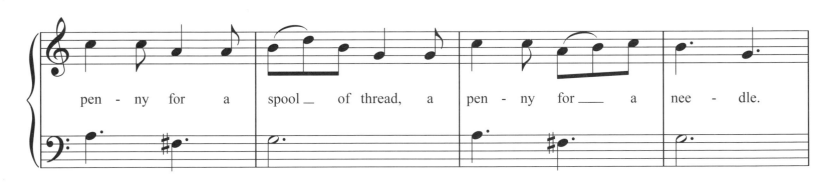

pen - ny for a spool ___ of thread, a pen - ny for ___ a nee - dle.

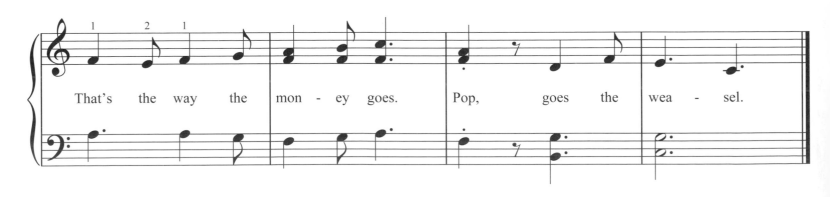

That's the way the mon - ey goes. Pop, goes the wea - sel.

SMILE
Theme from MODERN TIMES

Words by JOHN TURNER
and GEOFFREY PARSONS
Music by CHARLES CHAPLIN

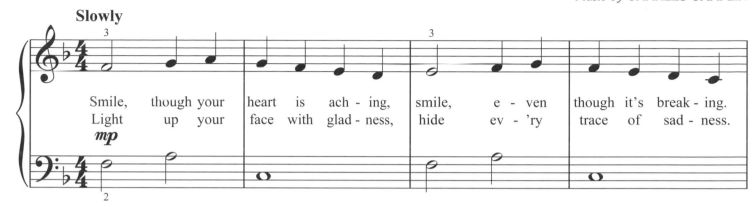

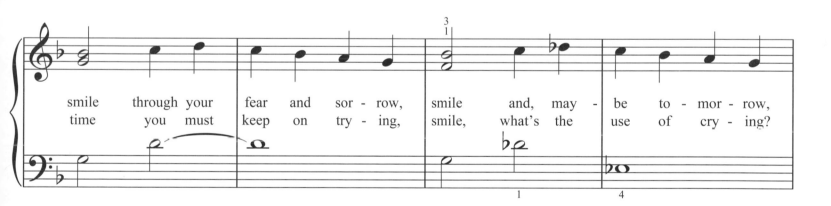

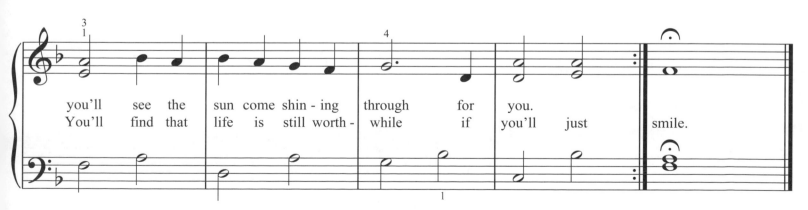

PUFF THE MAGIC DRAGON

Words and Music by LENNY LIPTON
and PETER YARROW

Moderately

Puff the mag - ic drag - on lived by the sea and

frol - icked in the au - tumn mist in a land called Hon - a - lee.

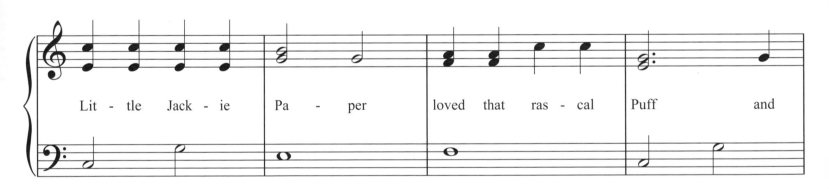

Lit - tle Jack - ie Pa - per loved that ras - cal Puff and

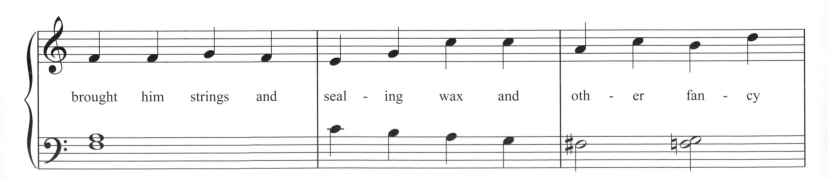

brought him strings and seal - ing wax and oth - er fan - cy

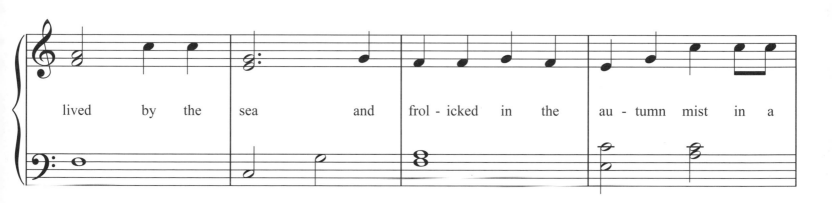

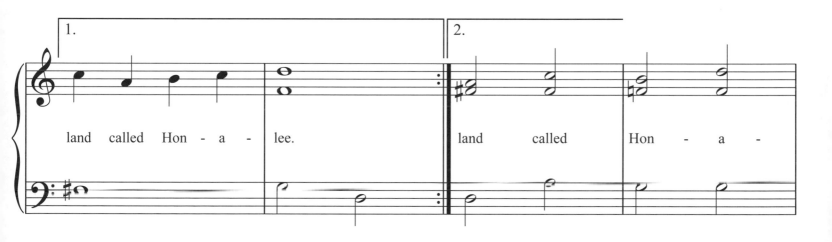

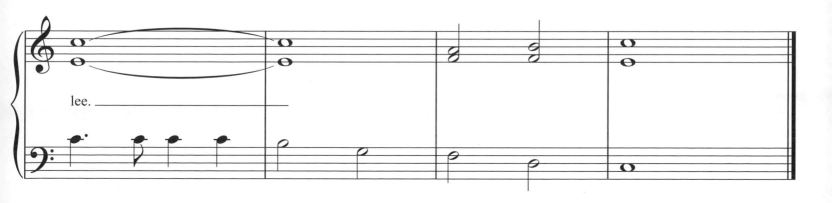

SATIN DOLL
from SOPHISTICATED LADIES

Words by JOHNNY MERCER
and BILLY STRAYHORN
Music by DUKE ELLINGTON

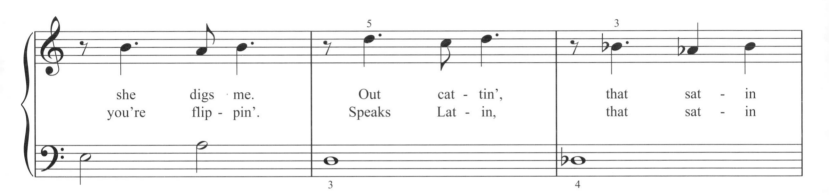

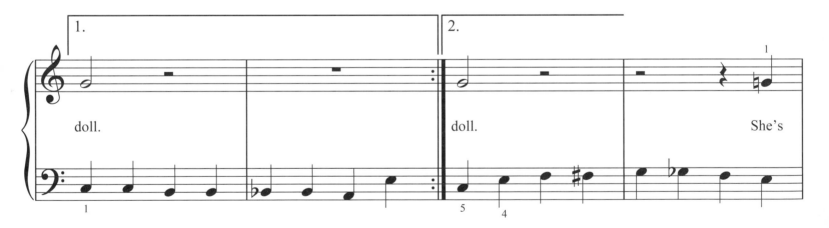

I'll give it a whirl, but I ain't for no girl catch - ing

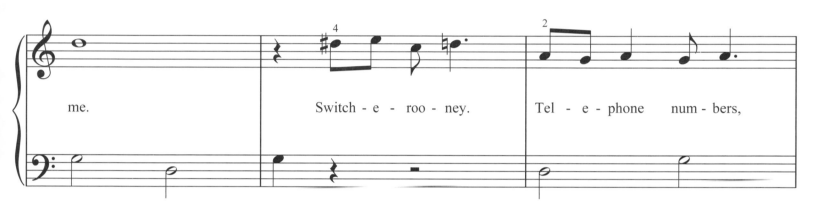

me. Switch - e - roo - ney. Tel - e - phone num - bers,

well, you know. Do - ing my rhum - bas, with u - no,

and that 'n' my sat - in doll.

SMOKE GETS IN YOUR EYES

from ROBERTA

Words by OTTO HARBACH
Music by JEROME KERN

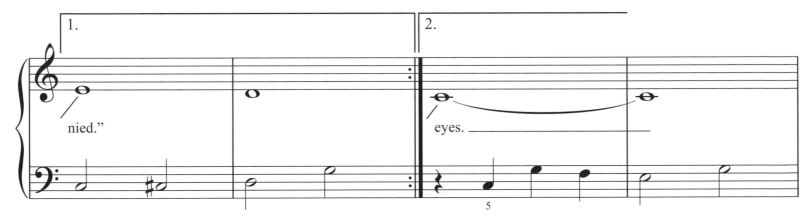

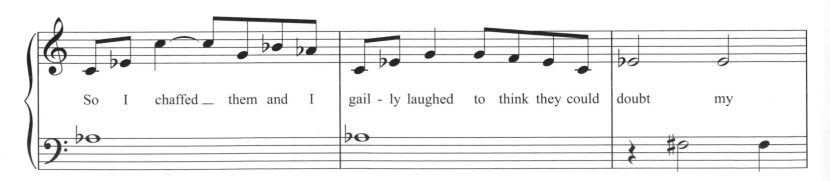

love.   Yet to-day,_____ my love has   flown a - way._____ I am with-

out   my   love.   Now   laugh-ing friends de - ride,   tears I can - not

hide. _____   So I smile and   say,   "When a   love - ly flame

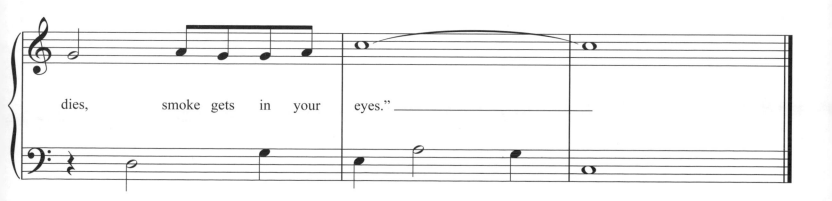

dies,   smoke gets in your   eyes." _____

SOMEWHERE OUT THERE
from AN AMERICAN TAIL

Music by BARRY MANN
and JAMES HORNER
Lyric by CYNTHIA WEIL

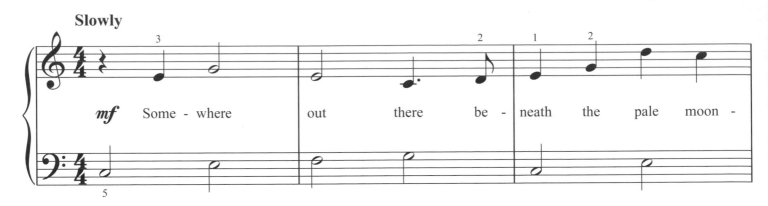

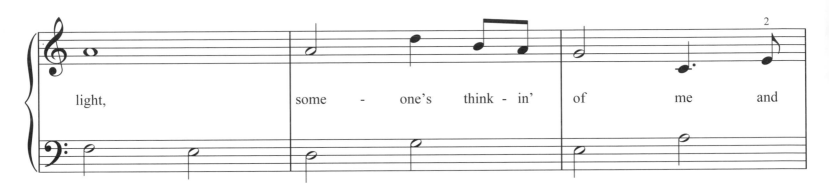

we'll find one an - oth - er in that big some - where out

there. And e - ven though I know how ver - y far a - part we are, it

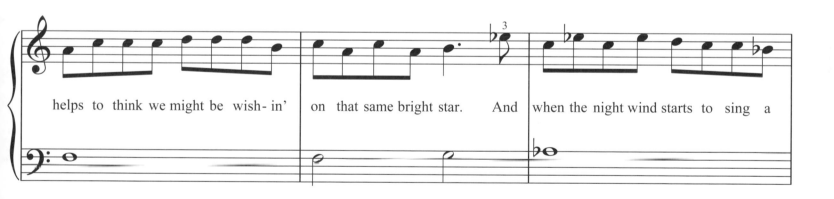

helps to think we might be wish - in' on that same bright star. And when the night wind starts to sing a

lone - some lul - la - by, it helps to think we're sleep - ing un - der -

neath the same big sky. *rit.* Some - where *a tempo* out there, if

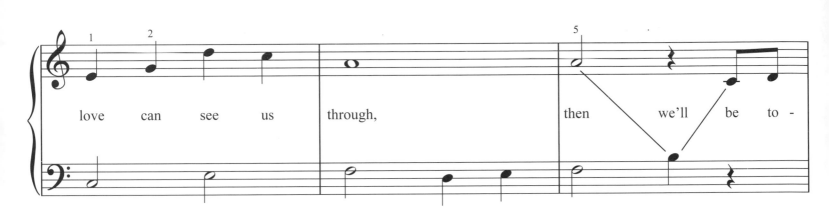

love can see us through, then we'll be to -

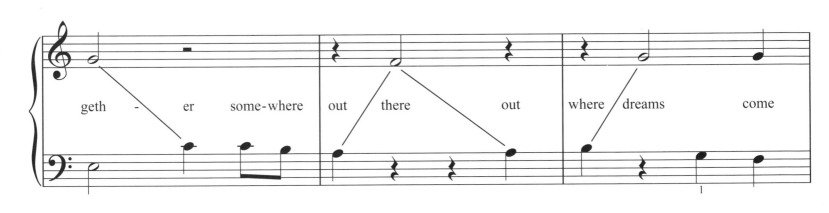

geth - er some-where out there out where dreams come

true. _____ *rit.*

SUPERCALIFRAGILISTIC-EXPIALIDOCIOUS

from Walt Disney's MARY POPPINS

Words and Music by RICHARD M. SHERMAN
and ROBERT B. SHERMAN

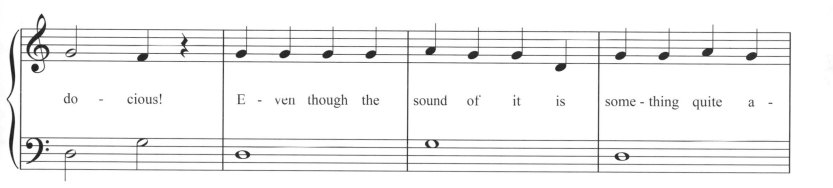

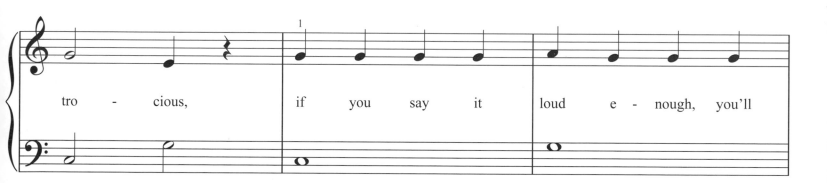

ex - pi - al - i - do - cious! Um did - dle did - dle did - dle,

um did - dle ay! Um did - dle did - dle did - dle, um did - dle ay! Be -

cause I was a - fraid to speak when I was just a lad, me

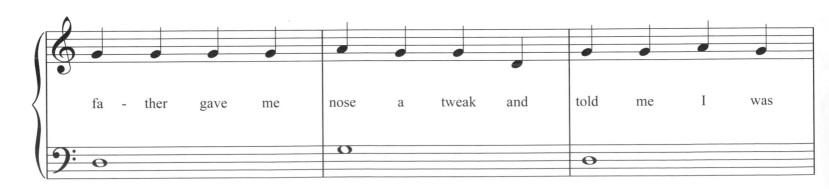

fa - ther gave me nose a tweak and told me I was

bad.   But   then   one   day   I   learned   a   word   that

saved   me   ach - in'   nose.   The   big - gest   word   you   ev - er   heard   and

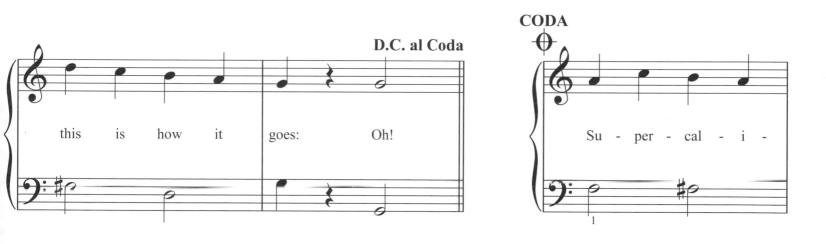

D.C. al Coda   **CODA**

this   is   how   it   goes: Oh!   Su - per - cal - i -

frag - il - is - tic - ex - pi - al - i - do - cious!

STAR WARS
(Main Theme)
from STAR WARS, THE EMPIRE STRIKES BACK and RETURN OF THE JEDI

Music by JOHN WILLIAMS

Majestically

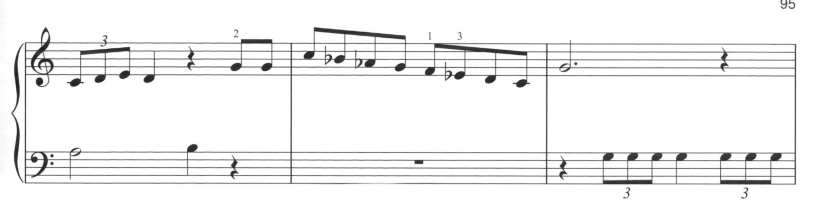

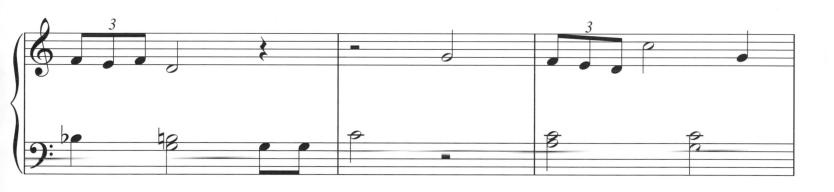

TEARS IN HEAVEN

Words and Music by ERIC CLAPTON
and WILL JENNINGS

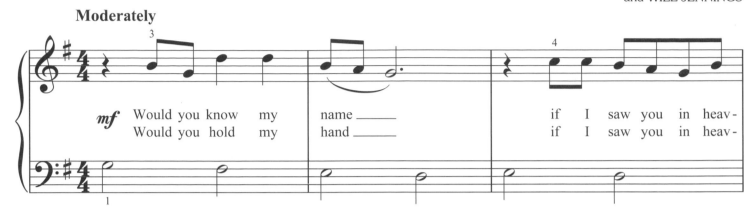

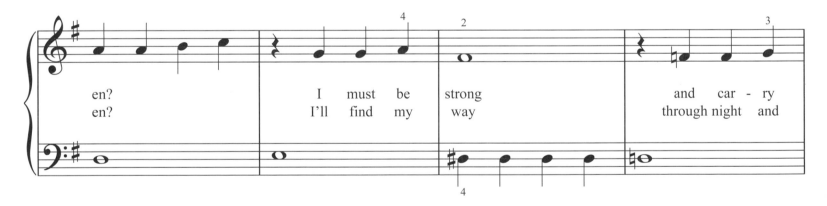

Time can bring you down, ___ time can bend your knees.

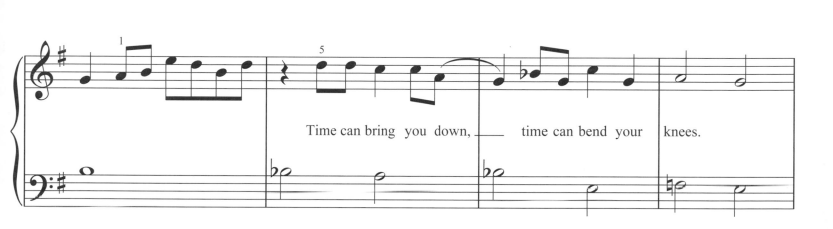

Time can break the heart, ___ have you beg - gin' please, beg-gin' please. ___

Instrumental

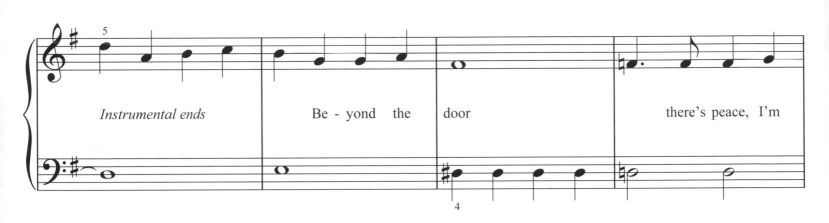

Instrumental ends   Be - yond the door   there's peace, I'm

D.C. al Coda
(verse 1)

sure.   And I   know there'll be   no more _____ tears in heav - en.

CODA

en.

TWINKLE, TWINKLE LITTLE STAR

Traditional

Gently, with motion

Twin - kle, twin - kle, lit - tle star; how I won - der

what you are. Up a - bove the world so high,

like a dia - mond in the sky! Twin - kle, twin - kle,

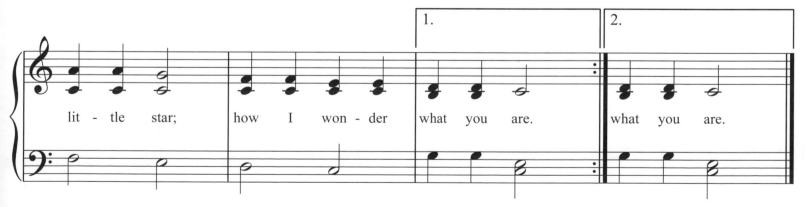

lit - tle star; how I won - der what you are. what you are.

TOMORROW

from the Musical Production ANNIE

Lyric by MARTIN CHARNIN
Music by CHARLES STROUSE

Moderately

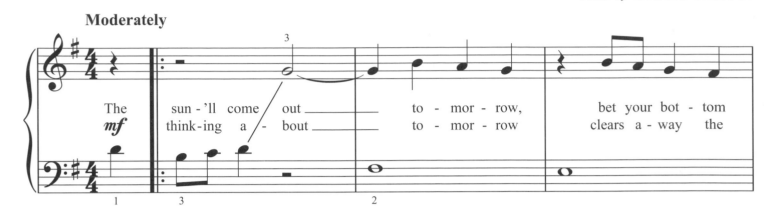

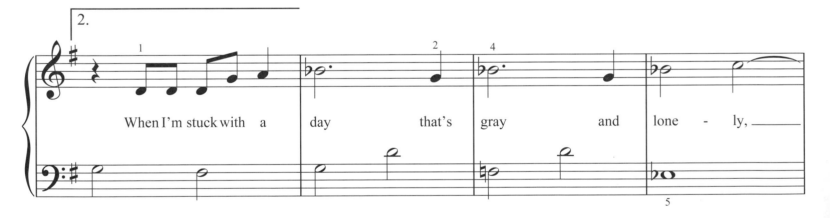

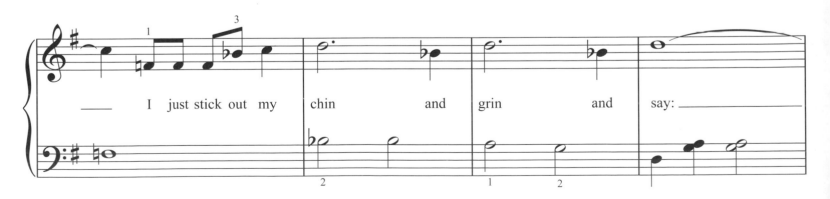

The sun - 'll come out _____

_____ to - mor - row, so you got to hang on till to - mor - row, _____ come what

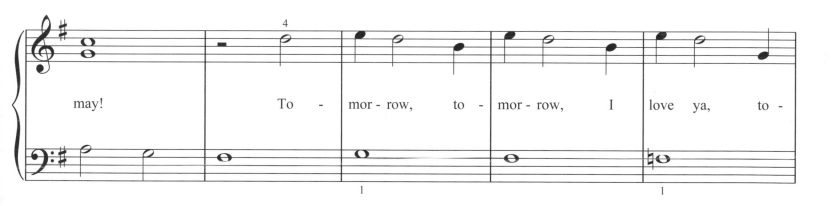

may! To - mor - row, to - mor - row, I love ya, to -

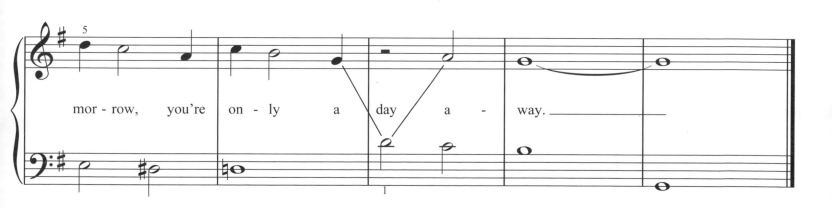

mor - row, you're on - ly a day a - way. _____

The Way You Look Tonight

from SWING TIME

Words by DOROTHY FIELDS
Music by JEROME KERN

Some - day when I'm aw - f'lly
love - ly, with your smile so
Love - ly, nev - er, nev - er

low, when the world is cold,
warm and your cheek so soft,
change, keep that breath - less charm.

I will feel a glow just think - ing of you
there is noth - ing for me but to love you
Won't you please ar - range it? 'Cause I love you

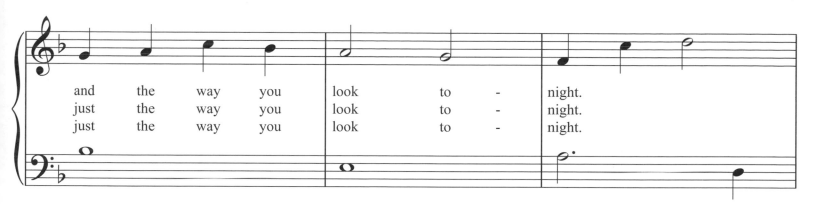

and the way you look to - night.
just the way you look to - night.
just the way you look to - night.

To Coda ⊕ | 1.

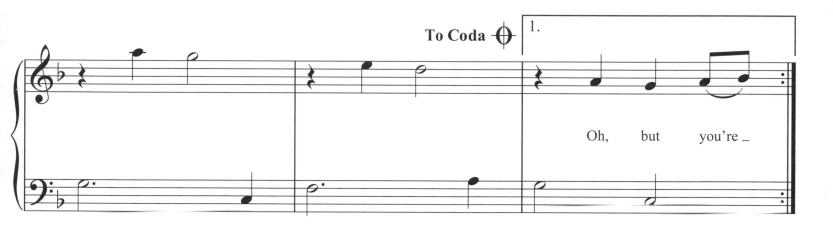

Oh, but you're

2.

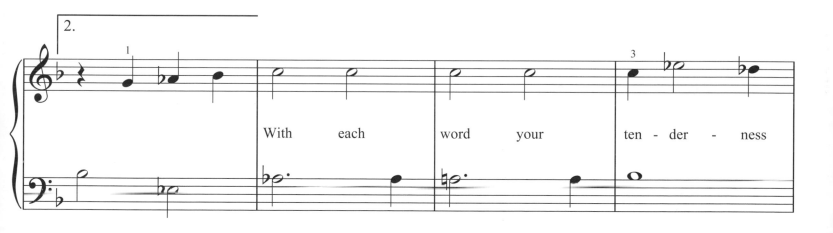

With each word your ten - der - ness

grows, tear - ing my fear a - part.

104

And that laugh, that wrin - kles your

nose touch - es my fool - ish heart. _____

D.C. al Coda

CODA

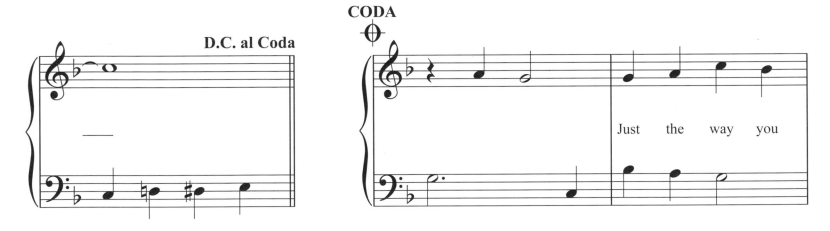

Just the way you

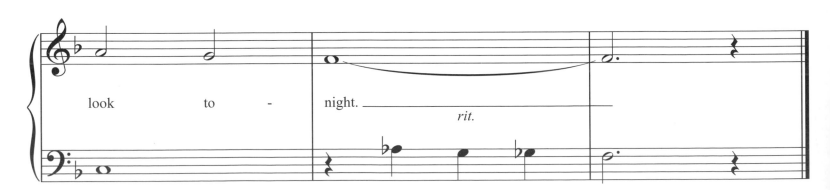

look to - night. _____

rit.

WHAT A WONDERFUL WORLD

Words and Music by GEORGE DAVID WEISS
and BOB THIELE

I see trees of green,
skies of blue,

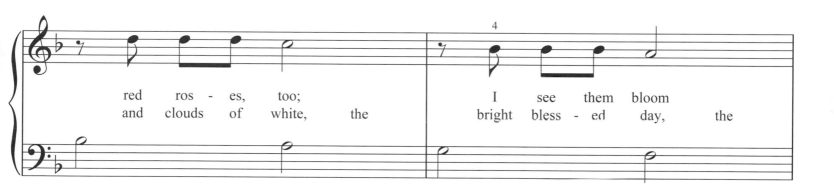

red ros - es, too; / I see them bloom
and clouds of white, the / bright bless - ed day, the

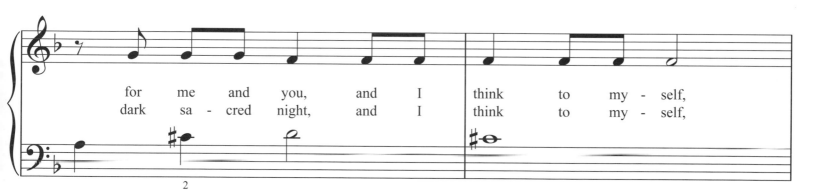

for me and you, and I / think to my - self,
dark sa - cred night, and I / think to my - self,

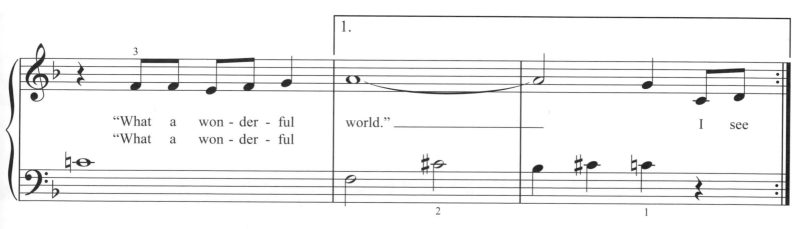

"What a won - der - ful world." / I see
"What a won - der - ful

world." _____ The col - ors of the rain - bow, so

pret - ty in the sky, are al - so on the fac - es of

peo - ple go - in' by. I see friends shak - in' hands, say - in', "How do you do?"

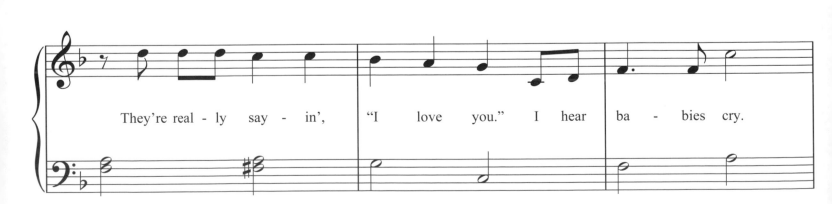

They're real - ly say - in', "I love you." I hear ba - bies cry.

I watch them grow. They'll learn much more than

I'll ev - er know, and I think to my - self, "What a won - der - ful

world," _____ yes, I think to my - self,

"What a won - der - ful world."
rit.

WHEN I FALL IN LOVE

Words by EDWARD HEYMAN
Music by VICTOR YOUNG

When I fall in love it will be for - ev - er,

or I'll nev - er fall in love. _____ In a

rest - less world like this is, love is end - ed be - fore it's be - gun, and too

man - y moon - light kiss - es seem to cool in the warmth of the sun.

When I give my heart it will be com - plete - ly,

or I'll nev - er give my heart. _____ And the

mo - ment I can feel that you feel that way too is

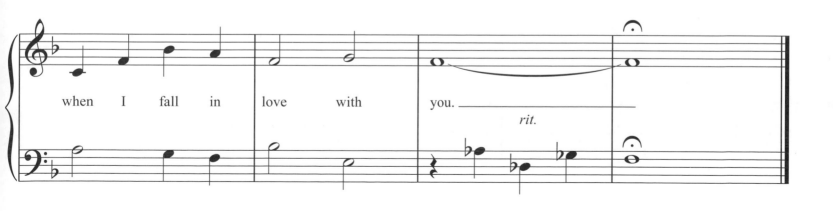

when I fall in love with you. _____ *rit.*

WHISTLE WHILE YOU WORK

Words by LARRY MOREY
Music by FRANK CHURCHILL

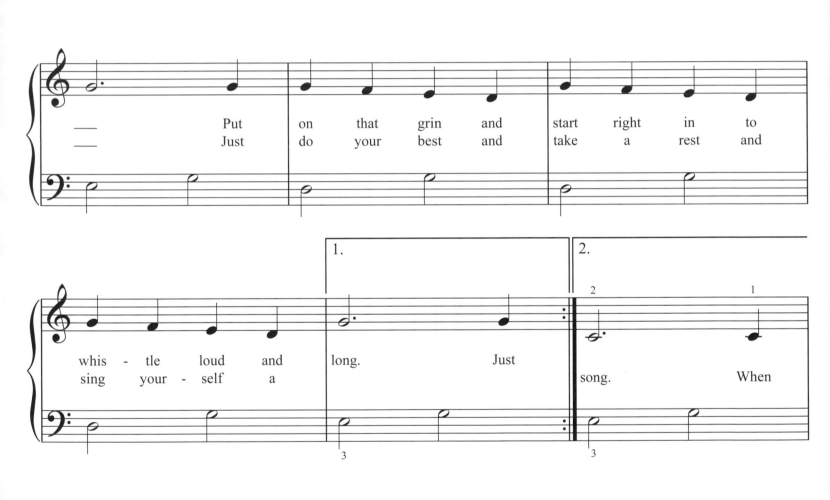

111

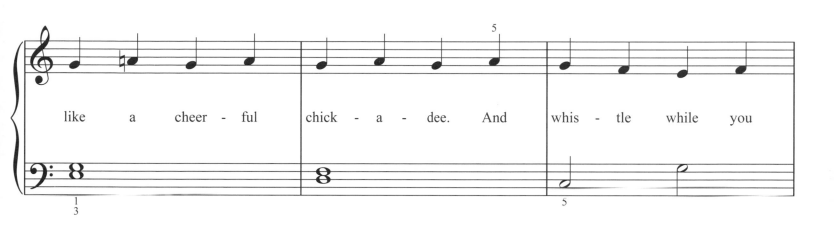

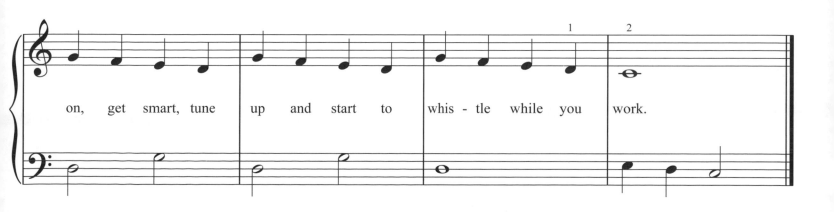

YANKEE DOODLE

Traditional

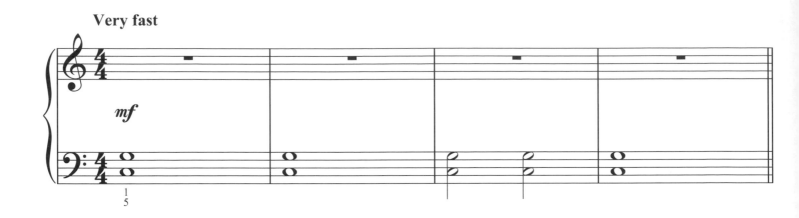

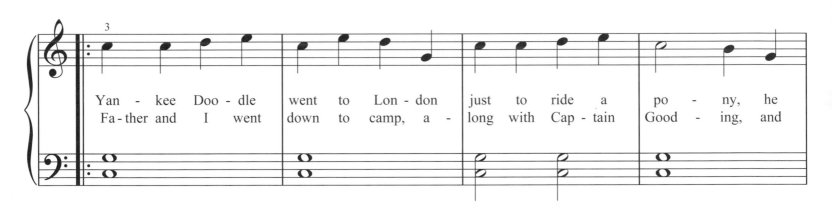

Yan - kee Doo - dle went to Lon - don just to ride a po - ny, he
Fa - ther and I went down to camp, a - long with Cap - tain Good - ing, and

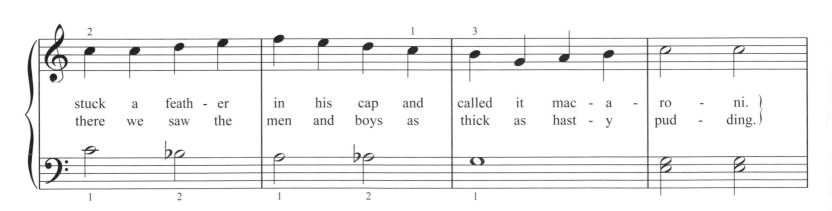

stuck a feath - er in his cap and called it mac - a - ro - ni. }
there we saw the men and boys as thick as hast - y pud - ding. }

Yan - kee Doo - dle, keep it up, Yan - kee Doo - dle dan - dy.

Mind the mu - sic and the step, and with the girls be hand - y.

1.

2.

With the girls be hand - y.

YESTERDAY

Words and Music by JOHN LENNON
and PAUL McCARTNEY

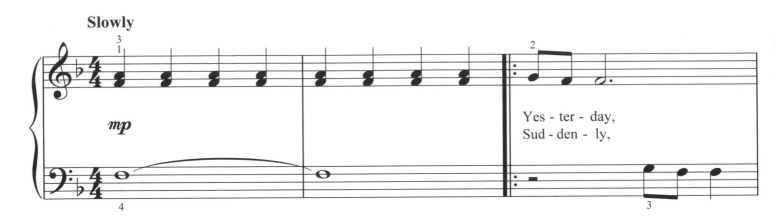

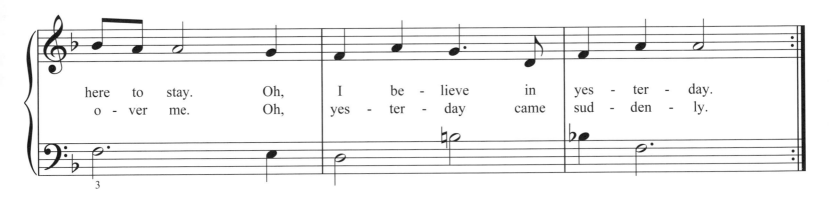

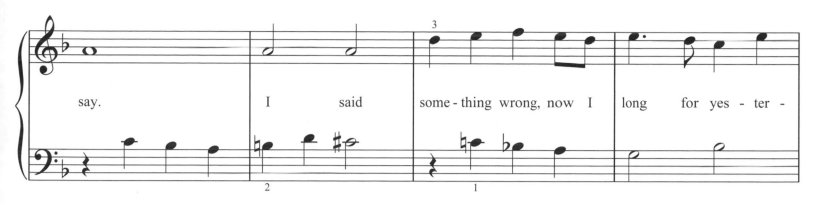

say.   I   said   some - thing wrong, now I   long   for yes - ter -

day.   Yes - ter - day,   love was such an eas - y

game to play.   Now I need a place to   hide a - way.   Oh,

I   be - lieve   in   yes - ter - day.   Hm. _____

rit.

ZIP-A-DEE-DOO-DAH

from Walt Disney's SONG OF THE SOUTH

Words by RAY GILBERT
Music by ALLIE WRUBEL

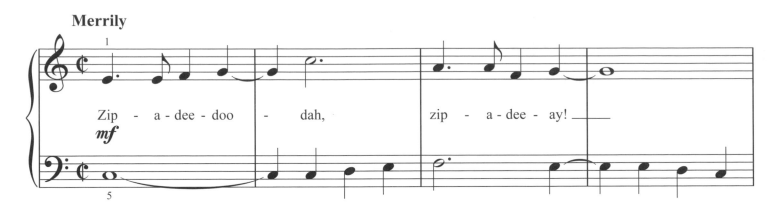

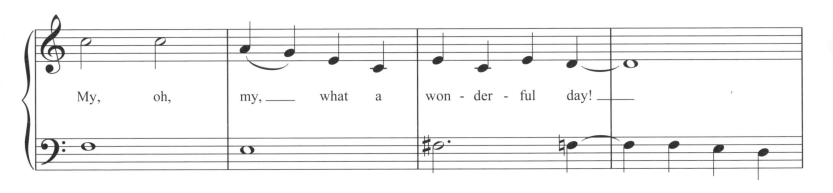

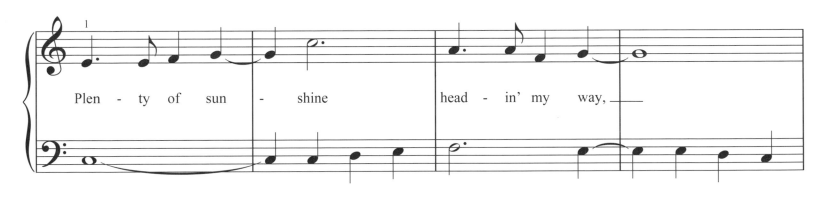

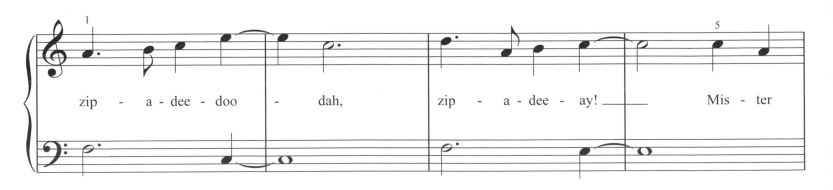

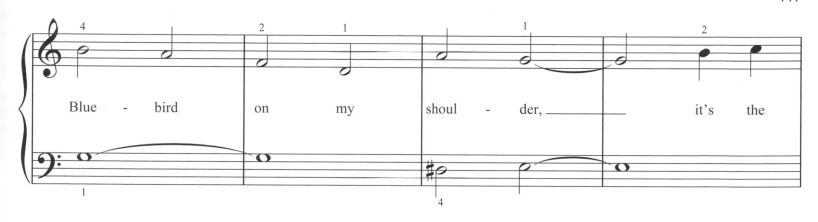

Blue - bird on my shoul - der, _____ it's the

truth, it's "act - ch'll," ev - 'ry - thing is "sat - is - fact - ch'll."

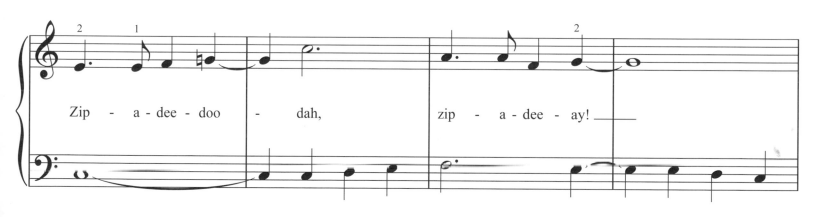

Zip - a - dee - doo - dah, zip - a - dee - ay! _____

Won - der - ful feel - ing, won - der - ful day. _____

A WHOLE NEW WORLD

from Walt Disney's ALADDIN

Music by ALAN MENKEN
Lyrics by TIM RICE

Moderately

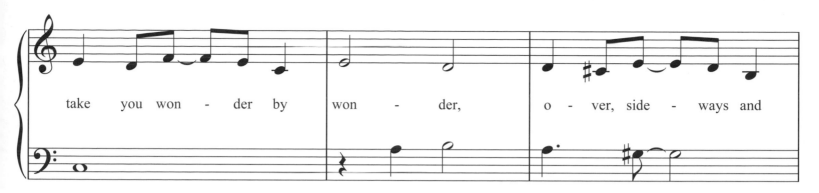

take you won - der by won - der, o - ver, side - ways and

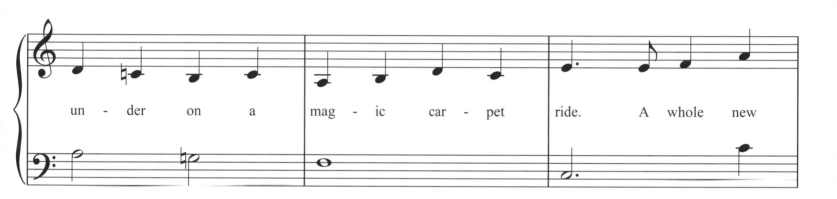

un - der on a mag - ic car - pet ride. A whole new

world, _____ a new fan - tas - tic point of

view. No one to tell us no, or where to go or

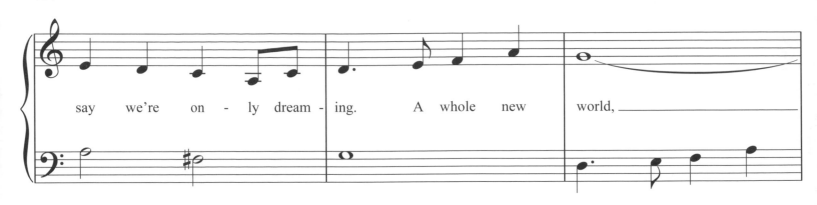

say we're on - ly dream - ing. A whole new world, _____

_____ a daz - zling place I nev - er knew. But when I'm

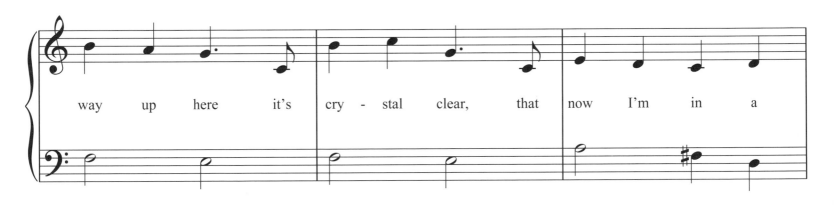

way up here it's cry - stal clear, that now I'm in a

whole new world with you.